MARX'S
Kapital
FOR BEGINNERS

Das
Kapital

David Smith
& Phil Evans

Pantheon Books, New York

6-21-94

I dedicate my share of this book to Laura, with love.
Friends deserving warmest thanks include: Dean
Manders, Larry Goldman, Violet.Smith, Elliot Smith,
Laurel Kerrihard, and Scott Kerrihard.

David Smith

- and my share of this book is for Polly.
Phil Evans

Library of Congress Cataloging in Publication Data

Smith, David N., 1952-
    Marx's Kapital for beginners.
    1. Marx, Karl, 1818-1883. Kapital.   I. Evans, Phil.   II. Marx, Karl, 1818-1883.
Kapital.   III. Title.
HB501 .S62   1983   335.4'1   82-47946
ISBN 0-394-71265-X   AACR2

Manufactured in the United States of America

First American Edition

About the Author and Illustrator

David Smith received his degree in economics from the
University of California at Berkeley and, at present, lives
in San Francisco.

Phil Evans, a British artist, is the illustrator of *Trotsky for
Beginners*.

Karl Marx

1. COMMODITIES P. 30.
Marx explains that the wealth of capitalist society is made up of a vast accumulation of commodities. How the commodity leads a strange 'double life'.

2. PRODUCTS FOR USE P. 34
Before the advent of capitalism production was for use – not for exchange. Aristotle explains.

3. ALIENATION OF USE-VALUE P. 37
The drive for profit clashes with human needs. Objects are misused.

4. OVERPRODUCTION P. 41
The capitalist market becomes 'glutted'. Capitalism destroys its surplus. Safety at work is subordinated to sales.

5.
EXCHANGE VALUE P. 44
Aristotle grapples with the problem of exchange. Marx points out that human labour is the basis for prices.

6. ABSTRACT LABOUR P. 47
Capitalism introduces the idea of 'abstract labour'. Everything is measured in terms of an 'average' labour norm.

7. ALIENATION OF USEFUL LABOUR P. 54
Abstract labour is not a material substance. Like a king's, its power comes only from general social recognition. There are no commodities in nature.

8. FETISHISM P. 57
Capitalism imbues commodities with magical powers. But revolutionaries challenge mysticism and all authoritarianism.

9. MONEY P.64
Money is the standard measure of the value of all commodities. Gold is the most powerful form of money. Ben Jonson reflects on riches.

10. THE ACCUMULATION OF CAPITAL P. 69
Capital generates profit. Marx solves the problem of how surplus value is extracted. The C-M-C and M-C-M cycles. Effects of competition. The capitalist discovers a value-creating commodity.

11. LABOUR-POWER P.86
Capital turns human labour into a commodity. Buyers -the bourgeoisie- and sellers - the workers- appear on the market.

12. EXPROPRIATION P. 89
Capitalism seizes the land, raw materials and machinery from the producers. The dispossessed are forced to sell their labour.

13. A HISTORY LESSON P. 92
Capitalism is born in England. But previous societies were also oppressive. Armed classes of owners controlled surplus labour.

14. THE MAKING OF THE WORKING CLASS P. 97
Henry VIII takes the land from the peasantry. They are replaced by sheep. Elizabeth I remarks on pauperism. In the towns the landless lose all control of production.

15. SURPLUS VALUE P. 113
Engels explains the secret of surplus value. Women reproduce labour-power. The difference between variable and constant capital.

16. THE RATE OF SURPLUS VALUE P. 129
A mathematical proof of capitalist crisis. The organic composition of capital. Speed-up. The rate of profit tends to fall. Wars help the capitalist. The struggle over the working day.

17. LABOUR-POWER AND CLASS STRUGGLE P. 147
How much do workers 'need'? Differing opinions. Wages reflect the balance of class power. Imperialism divides the world's workers.

18. ABOLITION OF WAGE-LABOUR P. 162
Workers' self-rule and communism. Abolition of the wage system. Feudal, slave, and wage labour. The 'fair wage' myth. The revolutionary party. Lessons of the Paris Commune. The expropriators are expropriated. Freedom.

Karl Marx was born in Trier, Germany, near the French border, in 1818. This was just after the Napoleonic wars, one year before **David Ricardo** published his pathbreaking work, *The Principles of Political Economy.*

CONGRATULATIONS, MRS MARX — HE'S A **CAPITAL** LITTLE CHAP!

DAVID RICARDO 1772–1823

The industrial revolution was well underway (Watt had invented the steam engine in 1769) and factory production was sweeping Europe.

After receiving a doctorate in philosophy from the University of Jena, Marx soon turned to revolutionary politics. He arrived at the conclusion that capitalism oppresses and exploits working people. Analysing *how* this happens, and organising working people to replace capitalism with communism, became Marx's lifelong preoccupation.

Marx remained an ardent revolutionary until his death in 1893. He never wavered in his conviction that the working class can—and must—abolish production for profit, and build, instead, a society based on 'freely associated labour' engaged in production for use.

Ueue
Rheinische Zeitung

Organ der Demokratie.

№ 301.   Köln, Samstag, den 19. Mai.   1840.

LEFT HAND DOWN A BIT

GEORGE HEGEL   LUDWIG FEUERBACH

(THERE IS AN INDEX AT THE BACK OF THIS BOOK)

Though **Capital** was Marx's life-work—a gigantic multi-volumed project started in the mid-1840's and never completely finished—Marx was hardly an armchair revolutionary.

DISCO DANCER IN GAS SLAYING
Newlywed killed at fuel pump

As editor of the *Rhenish Gazette* in 1842, in backward, absolutist Prussia, Marx (then only 24) was quickly immersed in politics. Already a radical philosopher—an exponent and critic of **Hegel** and **Feuerbach**—Marx was deeply impressed by an uprising of Silesian weavers, and by the misery and oppression of the Moselle wine-growers.

As a journalist, Marx *took* sides in the battles he reported, putting forward a radical defence of the rebel Silesian weavers and strongly arguing for their democratic rights.

HE CAMPAIGNED FOR THE AGE-OLD RIGHT OF PEASANTS TO PICK UP WOOD IN FORESTS—A RIGHT THREATENED BY A NEW BILL

The Prussian authorities grew increasingly unhappy with Marx, deciding, after several months, to suppress the *Rhenish Gazette* altogether. So dramatic was this turn of events in the eyes of Marx's German contemporaries that Marx became a celebrity of sorts—shown in one editorial cartoon as the mythical **Prometheus,** chained to a rock in punishment for stealing the fire of the gods —to share with suffering humankind.

Marx became both a celebrity and an exile. The Prussians unceremoniously booted him out.

WILLIAM WEITLING

PIERRE-JOSEPH PROUDHON

From this point on, Marx's odyssey begins. Expelled from Germany, Marx went to France—where he was again expelled ... to wind up, finally, in England, years later.

FREDERICK
ENGELS

JENNY
MARX

In France, Marx converted to
socialism. The first fruits of
Marx's initial foray into
economics included *The Holy
Family*, published in
collaboration with **Frederick
Engels** in 1843.

12

In 1845, Marx signed a contract for 'a book of economics'. Thinking he would finish this book quickly, Marx little realised that the project would soon grow out of hand. It would get bigger and bigger ...

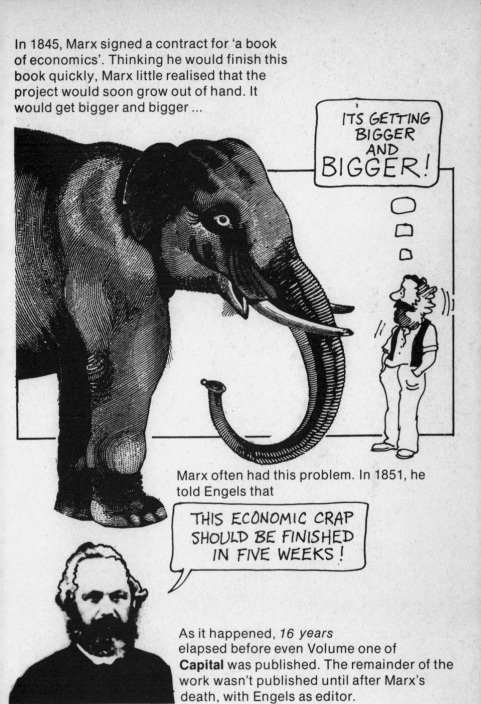

ITS GETTING BIGGER AND BIGGER!

Marx often had this problem. In 1851, he told Engels that

THIS ECONOMIC CRAP SHOULD BE FINISHED IN FIVE WEEKS!

As it happened, *16 years* elapsed before even Volume one of **Capital** was published. The remainder of the work wasn't published until after Marx's death, with Engels as editor.

Soon after Marx began his intensive work on economics, Karl and Jenny were thrown out of France—as 'politically undesirable' aliens.

POLITICALLY UNDESIRABLE

EXP...

VISA REF

VERB

NO ENTRY

DEPORTED

PERSONA NON GRATA

Moving to Brussels, Marx joined the secret League of the Just, a radical workers'organisation which soon changed its name to the *Communist League.* Engels joined, too. After completing his first published work on the capitalist economy—an essay against Proudhon entitled *The Poverty of Philosophy* (1847)— Marx was asked to collaborate with Engels on *The Manifesto of the Communist League,* better known as *The Communist Manifesto.* This incomparably famous pamphlet, encapsulating Marx and Engels' theory of the class struggle, was issued in 1848, 'the year of revolutions'.

14

Revolutions broke out in France, Germany, Hungary and elsewhere in 1848. They were revolutions of the rising capitalist class against feudal reaction, combined with revolts of artisans and workers. Marx and Engels rushed back to Germany to publish the *New Rhenish Gazette.*

OOH-ER! A DESPERATE BAND OF ARMED MEN!

NEW RHENISH GAZETTE! CLASS WAR — LATEST RESULTS!

It was in the pages of this revolutionary democratic newspaper that Marx published the series of lectures he had first delivered in 1847, *'Wage-Labour and Capital'.*

15

After the defeat of the revolution in Germany, Marx went on trial for sedition. After a stirring speech to the jury, Marx was acquitted.

Even so, Karl and Jenny were booted out of Germany again. This time, they went to England, where Engels settled, too. (His father owned a factory in Manchester.)

Marx began 12 years of work as foreign correspondent for the *New York Herald Tribune* and several other newspapers, including the *Vienna Presse*.

At first, Marx and Engels tried to keep the Communist League alive, but they soon decided it was no longer useful. Without a mass movement to sustain it, the group was becoming an émigré sect, splitting hairs in political isolation.

Marx devoted himself to journalism and the study of capitalism

SPLIT HARE

In 1858, Marx's studies had progressed to the point that he was able to draft a 1,400-page outline of his entire projected 'critique of political economy'. This outline, known as the *Grundrisse,* is a major work in its own right, presaging most of the themes in **Capital.** It is a *tour de force* of incomparable breadth and insight.

In 1859, Marx published *A Contribution to the Critique of Political Economy,* summarizing some of the basic ideas developed in the *Grundrisse*. This is an extremely valuable prologue to **Capital,** far more important for the understanding of Marx's 'theory of value' than is often realized. It is even more thorough than **Capital** on the question of money ....

In 1865, as a leading member of the General Council of the *International Workingman's Association* (which had formed the year before to be a formidable force), Marx replied at length to an argument against strikes by a Council member, **John Weston**, a carpenter.

DON'T COME CRYING TO US WHEN **YOU** FIND YOURSELF ON STRIKE, WESTON!

Marx's reply, later published in pamphlet form by his daughter **Eleanor,** expresses in a concise form many of his most vital ideas. These ideas won general approval in the IWA (perhaps better known as the 'First International').

ELEANOR MARX

VALUE, PRICE, AND PROFIT

At long last, in 1867, Volume One of **Das Kapital** rolled off the presses, to be greeted immediately and warmly in the workers' press. The capitalist press ignored it entirely.

WHAT'S THAT YOU'RE READING?

MARX'S CAPITAL— YOU SHOULD GET A COPY!

I WILL— BUT I HAVEN'T FINISHED THE GRUNDRISSE YET!

Marx felt that he had reached an important milestone with the publication of **Das Kapital,** placing a necessary theoretical weapon in the hands of the workers' movement. In Volume One, Marx demonstrates that capitalism is based on the *exploitation* of working women, men, and children. All the basic facts of modern society are analysed, from prices and profits to wages and the working day. Why labour products are 'commodities,' why money is so all-powerful, where capital originates and why economic crises happen—all these Marx analyses with searching care.

Engels had, indeed, been busy promoting **Capital**, as had others in the International. Still, **Das Kapital** didn't sell very briskly at first. Karl's mother, **Henrietta,** complained:

(*THIS IS WHAT MARX ADVISED HIS FRIEND FRANZISKA KUGELMANN)

HITHERTO UNPUBLISHED FRAGMENT OF MARX'S LOST DIARIES.

Woken at 11 o'clock this morning by an infernal ringing on the door bell. After a time Jenny came up, very irritable, with a final demand from the butcher. Nothing is more distasteful than the sight of the petty bourgeoisie in the act of primitive accumulation...

Rose at 12. Fearful headache for some reason, and Jenny very distant. Sitting at my desk very uncomfortable on account of boils being troublesome. When I complained Jenny said something I didn't quite catch about 'sitting on my backside all day' and 'honest day's work'. My papers all in a fearful mess, but couldn't think why.

Over lunch - vegetarian of necessity owing to the business with the butcher - it all came out. When Fred came back with me from the meeting last night he made what Jenny calls 'a fearful racket' - though I can't say I noticed at the time, as we were both rather jolly. He broke the drawing-room tongs showing us his artillery strategy to defend Paris against the Prussians. He also picked up the manuscript of Volume One and threw it into the air shouting 'Down with words! Words - Pah! We need guns!' (That explains the mess.) I was just going to point out that Fred is at heart a decent fellow, with a fine grasp of the dialectic, but tends to get over-excited, when the doorbell went again. Peeping out - as we are obliged to do these days - I was horrified to see a constable on the doorstep! Jenny answered and I heard snatches of what passed. 'Did a little foreign gentleman (!) with a big beard live here? Did he have a friend? When would he be back? Then there was something about '45 shillings worth of damage to the street lamps in Tottenham Court Road'.

At last he went away. I said something about the class role of functionaries in the service of the state apparatus but was met with an icy silence. Suddenly there was a shout in the hall and who should come in - with the worst possible timing - but Fred, with a bottle of Sherry in each hand! He clapped them down on the table very boisterously and said 'What was that big fat Bobby doing coming down the street?' Had Jenny been robbing banks?

At this point I am afraid Jenny made an unpleasant scene. She shouted 'There IS a spectre haunting Europe - you two!' and flounced out of the room, crying. Fred was put out for a moment, but then slapped me on the back, cried out 'That's the Holy Family for you!' and was good enough to lend me five shillings before carrying me off to the tavern at the Angel to meet the comrades...

n 1871, the PARIS COMMUNE took place! A spectacular uprising of Parisian workers and small independent producers occurred during the Franco-Prussian war of 1870. Bitterly discontented with the repressive regime of the first emperor Napoleon's adventurer nephew, Louis Napoleon Bonaparte, the workers of Paris decided to take their lives into their own hands.

In March 1871 the Parisian working people toppled the government and seized the reins of power. By means of energetic, determined, and radically democratic measures, these working men and women reconstituted Paris as a socialist commune.

'THEY STORMED THE GATES OF HEAVEN. WHAT INITIATIVE, WHAT ELASTICITY, WHAT HEROISM THESE PARISIANS HAVE SHOWN! '

Speaking for the International, Marx declared the Paris Commune the first example of 'the dictatorship of the proletariat'. He meant the working class ruling itself democratically, in its own name, while fighting off the counter-revolutionary efforts of the displaced capitalist class.

'THE BEST THING ABOUT THE COMMUNE WAS ITS OWN WORKING EXISTENCE: ITS DEMOCRATIC PROCEDURES, THE STEPS TAKEN TOWARDS THE ABOLITION OF PRIVATE PROPERTY, THE CREATION OF REAL WORKING COOPERATION BETWEEN PRODUCERS...'

But now something unusual in military annals took place. After two glorious months of the Commune, the French and Prussian armies—once at each other's throats—harbouring not the slightest tender feelings for one another—united to oppose the Parisian workers. Before long, the military effort to overwhelm the Commune met with success. A White Terror much more brutal than the terror of the French Revolution of 1793 followed. More than a hundred thousand Communards were killed. Thousands more were exiled.

'Paris has been delivered. At last the fighting is over; order, work and security will reign once more.' Marshal MacMahon

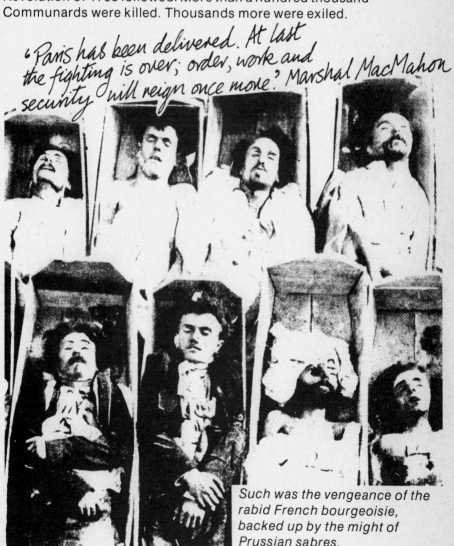

Such was the vengeance of the rabid French bourgeoisie, backed up by the might of Prussian sabres.

27

It was at this fateful juncture that Marx set about revising **Das Kapital** for a French translation. This appeared as a series of penny pamphlets, intended for Parisian working people, between 1872 and 1875.

Marx's French publisher, Lachâtre, was an exiled Communard. Marx's goal was to communicate his analysis of capitalism and the class struggle to the survivors of the Commune. He hoped that this would help them regroup and rethink their strategy.

Is **Das Kapital** an obscure, lifeless, esoteric work?

No.

Capital is for everyone who works for a living in the shadow of a boss. It argues that capitalism is a world system based on wage-labour. The relevance of Marx's **Capital** grows as wage-labour extends into all corners of the earth.

1.
COMMODITIES

People *make* commodities; *sell* commodities; *buy* commodities. That's what the hustle and bustle is all about.

ANYTHING PRODUCED FOR EXCHANGE IS A COMMODITY!

Every day, on every side, we encounter an immense accumulation of commodities. All these worldly things— ready for sale, waiting to tempt money from our pockets, are 'commodities', bearing odious, white paper labels with familiar symbols.

This is how commodities appear—with prices on their foreheads, talking dollars and cents. The price tag is the unique insignia of the commodity.

This accumulation of commodities; this mass of objects bearing price tags—this we may call THE WEALTH OF CAPITALIST SOCIETY.

$27

THE COMMODITY
AS AN ODDITY

'The commodity is an oddity because it leads a *double life*. It is a product of labour made not just for **use**, but for **exchange**. 'For sale', the product acquires a quality not present in nature—*exchangeability*. As a commodity, it is not only *useful* but *exchangeable*.

Furs, for example, can be used either to protect us from the cold—or to attract money. Spices can flavour our food—or sell for a price. Here we have the unique feature of the product as a commodity. It has two dimensions: both *what it is*, and what it is *worth*. The commodity is not just an *object*, but an object with a *price*.

In the language of the early economists, we
may say with **Adam Smith,** that:

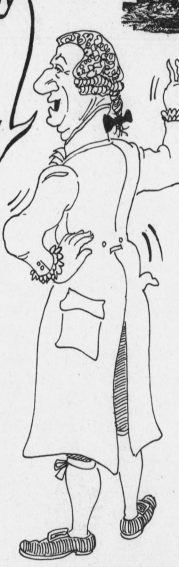

A Commodity
if both a
ufe value
and a value!

GOODNESS ME —
HOW DIFFICULT!
AND ALL I WANTED
WAS A PAIR OF
SOCKS!

To grasp value we must fully understand the relationship between use-value and value.

Together, use-value and value are the twin sides of the commodity—they are the opposite poles of its double life.

'A use-value is anything outside us that we find necessary, useful, or pleasant. By the use of its properties, the useful thing allows us to satisfy some need or desire.'

There is surely no mystery here! As a useful product, the commodity is *not* an oddity. But the commodity is far more than a simple use-value.

A ROSE IS A ROSE IS A ROSE.

GERTRUDE STEIN

Materially useful as a use-value, the rose is *socially* useful *(exchangeable)* as a commodity. Fragrant and lovely, the rose also sells for a dollar, and trades for a handful of chocolates.

In a nutshell the commodity is valuable both for *use* and for *exchange*.

33

2. PRODUCTS FOR USE

Before capitalism began (in Europe in the 15th century) and even afterwards (until quite recently, in fact), production in most parts of the world was production for *use*. Dresses were made to be *worn*, not *sold*. Chocolates were made to be *eaten*, not *exchanged*. *Only with the ascent of capitalism did production for exchange become predominant.*

During the lifetime of Aristotle—circa 220 B.C.—commerce was a lively but very minor part of overall economic life. *'Economics',* in fact, is the name Aristotle applied to production for use. Production for *exchange* Aristotle called 'Chrematistics.'

The same was true for slaveholding antiquity—in Egypt, Greece, Carthage, Rome, and elsewhere. Though slaves produced for the use of *others*—their masters—they seldom produced for exchange. Nor were commodities typically produced by European serfs, Chinese peasants, Indian patriarchal families, or working people of other pre-capitalist societies.

Use-value, not exchange-value, was the goal and result of pre-capitalist production. Indeed, producing to *sell* and *profit* was typically regarded as immoral, a perverse way of life inspired by greed, pride, gluttony, and vanity.

Only in capitalist society does exchangeability become an established feature of the labour product. *Only in capitalist society, thus, does the product lead a double life—as a* value *and a* use-value.

3. **ALIENATION OF USE-VALUE**

If we are fully to grasp capitalist production, we must recognize, above all, that the double life of the commodity is neither peaceful nor harmonious. On the contrary, value and use-value clash. The capitalist quest for profit—for ever greater sums of value—radically clashes with human desires for food, shelter, and other use-values.

THE CAPITALIST QUEST FOR PROFIT—FOREVER-GREATER SUMS OF VALUE CLASHES WITH HUMAN DESIRES FOR FOOD, SHELTER AND OTHER USE-VALUES

We are speaking now of the distortion, repression, and abuse of the product as a useful object—its misuse as *use-value*. To the extent that the product is treated as a value, it is *alienated* as a use-value.

'Mummy always chose my clothes until I discovered Smirnoff.'

The effect is shattering

SMIRNOFF

A commodity must be useful or seem useful if anyone is to buy it. But usefulness is not the main issue. As a *commodity*, the product must be *sold* to be used. Sale is the necessary and indispensable prerequisite for use. Without exchange, there can be no use. If a commodity should fail to demonstrate exchangeability, its usefulness, too, will be cancelled.

Thus does 'alien' exchange dominate 'natural' use.

Take a loaf of bread, for example. Sitting in a supermarket, its usefulness lies completely dormant. Though perfectly edible, it must prove its *exchange-value* before it can be eaten. If no one buys it, the bread will rot on the shelf—even though people starve.

The same is true for every commodity: NO SALE, NO USE. This is a principle of private property. Commodities are not made to be given away. Capitalists do not share with workers.

Another example of the distortion of use-value resulting from production for exchange is the *sabotage* of the product. Business cares about product quality only from the standpoint of sales. If sales are unaffected, business will happily cut costs by skimping on labour, safety precautions and materials, —typically making useless, dangerous, even deadly products. Are the following horrors unfamiliar?

- Cars 'unsafe at any speed'
- Baby formulas poisonous to infants
- Food shot up with carcinogens
- Nuclear power plants with sub-standard insulation
  - Medicine that kills

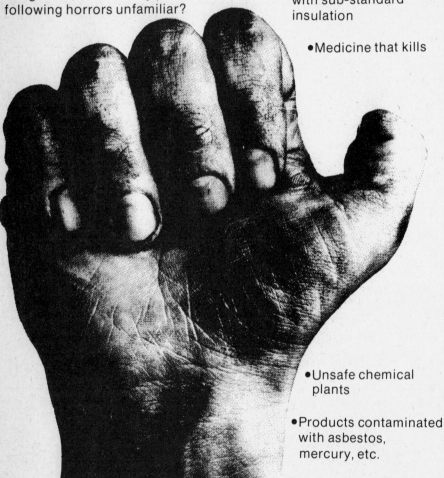

- Unsafe chemical plants
- Products contaminated with asbestos, mercury, etc.

And so it goes.

40

4. OVERPRODUCTION

Still another example of how exchange-value eclipses use-value is evident in so-called 'over-production'. Periodically, production results in what business regards as an 'excess' of commodities. The consequence is that prices and profits fall—to the chagrin and mortal fury of capitalists. The market, they say, is 'glutted'. To reverse matters, business intentionally and cheerfully destroys part of its product. Why? Simply to raise prices and profits. Never mind that people lack adequate housing, medical care, or food. From the profit-standpoint of business, the market 'glut' is a catastrophe. It must

be disposed of. *Not* by making surplus use-values freely *available* to people—heavens, no! Rather, by *destroying* them.

'SURPLUS' TOMATOES BEING BURNED IN THE U.S.

This is what happened, for example, during the Great Depression of the 1930s. Agribusiness found itself burdened with an 'excess' of pigs and milk, causing prices to fall. The result was that pigs were killed and milk disposed of, in vast quantities, to safeguard profits—though many went hungry. To keep profits *up*, supply is kept *down*. Production is restricted as a matter of course.

In the US, for example, barely 70% of the total productive capacity is used. Much of the general production apparatus remains idle—to say nothing of the millions of unemployed workers.

As we see, capitalism requires products universally endowed with exchangeability. Business places a premium not on what the object *is*, but on its *value*.

5. If value exists and appears only in exchange, it is imperative for us to grasp the meaning of exchange. Aristotle is once again a helpful guide.

CONSIDER AN EXCHANGE OF FIVE BEDS FOR ONE HOUSE. THESE PRODUCTS ARE NOT ALIKE. BEDS AND HOUSES HAVE DIFFERENT QUALITIES AND DIFFERENT USES. HOW, THEN, CAN THEY EXCHANGE AS EQUALS? ARE THEY REALLY EQUAL?

EXCHANGE

VALUE

NO! THOUGH EXCHANGING THEM SEEMS TO IMPLY THEIR EQUALITY, BEDS AND HOUSES ARE NOT REALLY EQUAL. THE APPEARANCE OF EQUALITY IS FALSE. IN REALITY, PEOPLE SIMPLY DECIDE TO EXCHANGE UNEQUAL THINGS.

However, Aristotle ultimately came to the conclusion that real equality between commodities is impossible. After all, Aristotle reasoned, no two objects are really the same. Though mistaken in his conclusion, Aristotle at least seriously grappled with the problem of 'equality' in exchange. This elevates him head and shoulders above most contemporary economists, who refuse even to consider the possibility that exchange embodies an inherent principle of equality.

That *just so much* (not more, not less) is the price of a commodity when supply and demand balance indicates that something else is the basis for this price.

If we agree with Aristotle that no two objects are exactly alike—and if they were, why would we exchange them?— we face a difficulty. How can objects that are materially unlike, with unlike properties, systematically exchange for each other in established proportions?

Imagine for a moment that there are just two objects in question—say, a deer and a beaver—and just two owners (both of them hunters). Suppose that it requires one day of hunting to capture a deer, but seven days to capture a beaver. If both hunters are equally skilful at catching both types of quarry, then parting with one beaver for one deer seems unreasonable. Why trade the product of seven day's labour for the product of one day's labour? Why hunt for seven days to wind up with a deer requiring only one day of hunting?

It *is* possible to make this exchange—what would prevent it? Any producer can make an unequal exchange either unwittingly or if s/he so desires. But the matter changes when we talk about *systematic* commodity exchange, that is, capitalism. Here, the principle that regulates commodity exchange is *labour-time*. Materially, commodities may be totally dissimilar—but they do have one thing in common: all require human effort for their production or appropriation. This provides a basis for exchange.

By this standard, seven deer are equal to one beaver. That is, each embodies an equal quantity of labour.

This raises a problem: what does it mean to say that a product 'embodies' labor?

Just this: that so much labour 'goes into' the product. In production, the material object existing before production changes. The body of the object changes with the labour expended upon it. This labour thus has 'bodily' results—it is *embodied* in a material thing.

Before work begins, the object already has a particular form derived from nature. Labour *adds* to this, changing the form of the object. In this way, the purpose guiding labour is 'objectified'—it *goes into* the object.

46

6. ABSTRACT LABOUR

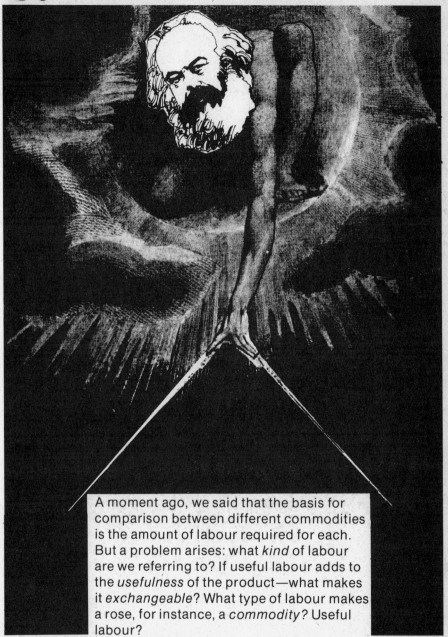

A moment ago, we said that the basis for comparison between different commodities is the amount of labour required for each. But a problem arises: what *kind* of labour are we referring to? If useful labour adds to the *usefulness* of the product—what makes it *exchangeable*? What type of labour makes a rose, for instance, a *commodity*? Useful labour?

No. That was **David Ricardo's** mistake. Brilliantly perceiving that value is *embodied labour,* Ricardo failed fully to analyse this proposition. Above all, Ricardo fell short of the concept of *abstract* labour ...

Though different kinds of labour are not materially equal, they can be *treated as if they were.* This is vital! This is the secret we've been seeking.

Materially unequal different forms of useful labour—say, watchmaking and bed-making—can be *treated as if they were equal,* to facilitate exchange. Activities involving different skills, different operations, and different tools can be treated as the *same*—so that the products of different activities can be regarded as equal.

In other words: USEFUL LABOUR can be treated as ABSTRACT LABOUR.

A USEFUL RICARDO

AN ABSTRACT RICARDO

Before exploring abstract labour in detail, it will be useful
to draw a preliminary contrast:

USEFUL LABOUR

Work activities as they really are with unique material qualities

Embodied in use-value

ABSTRACT LABOUR

Work activities *treated* as if they had *no* distinguishing qualities

Embodied in value

THERE IS NO ROYAL ROAD TO SCIENCE, AND ONLY THOSE WHO DO NOT DREAD THE FATIGUING CLIMB OF ITS STEEP PATHS HAVE A CHANCE OF GAINING ITS LUMINOUS SUMMITS. MY CONCEPT OF VALUE, IN PARTICULAR, REQUIRES SERIOUS STUDY.

BECAUSE IT'S THERE!

DAMN! I'VE DROPPED THE GRUNDRISSE!

When tailors and weavers exchange products, for example, they view their work not as it really is, but as work, pure and simple, as labour *per se*. Equating one coat to 20 yds of linen means equating *coatmaking* (the labour of a tailor) to *linenmaking* (the labour of a weaver). The *products* are equated—and so is the labour that *goes into* them. *Trading* products means *treating* them as *equal*.

COATS AND LINEN ARE DIFFERENT PRODUCTS —BUT THE LABOUR THAT PRODUCES THEM —

—CAN BE EQUATED. WHEN THEY'RE TRADED THEY'RE TREATED AS EQUAL !

Sans qualities, all labour is *alike.* X hours of one type of quality-less labour is equal to X hours of another type of quality-less labour. Thus, abstractness permits exchange. Equal quantities of abstract labour may exchange for one another. With the fact of exchange itself, abstract labour is certified as real. The product proves itself to be a commodity, an embodiment of value.

= × 5,000

Producers don't usually think to themselves 'Aha! By trading my watch for a bed, I simultaneously disregard the material qualities of both products, viewing them as qualitatively equal and thus rendering them the result not of useful but of abstract labour.'

But this is what people do .... whatever they may think.

When a palace is traded for so many tins of boot polish, the labour embodied in each is treated, *de facto,* as if it were identical to the other. The same is true when a volume of

ILL GIVE YOU 79 BILLION MILK BOTTLE TOPS FOR YOUR ROLLS-ROYCE MISTER!

DONE!

Shakespeare's works is exchanged for so many ounces of snuff. Clearly, the use-value of each product differs—and so does the useful labour corresponding to this use-value. *They are values.*

This means that the qualitatively *unequal* useful labour embodied in them is treated as qualitatively equal. When we exchange watches, dresses, beds or houses we disregard their material properties. The basis for this is that we disregard the material differences between *watchmaking, dressmaking, bed-making* and *house-building.* A certain number of watches— made of metal, jewels, and glass—are exchangeable for a certain number of beds—made of goosefeathers, wood, foam rubber and cloth—because the different kinds of *labour* required to assemble them *are treated as equal.*

It isn't that two kinds of labour lurk in the body of the commodity. Rather, the *useful* labour inherent in the product as a use-value can be treated as qualitatively abstract to facilitate exchange.

No matter how slowly you work, the commodity you produce contains only the amount of 'equal' labour-time that the *average* producer would expend. If you try to charge a price for your product on the basis of the exact, actual time it takes, you will soon discover that the *actual* time spent performing useful labour is not the point. It's how much socially *standard* labour—*abstract* labour—the product normally requires.

Average, equal labour is what people pay attention to—and it can change suddenly, for reasons independent of the nature of concrete, useful labour.

When the power-loom was introduced into England, for example, it halved the time required to make cloth. Hand-loom weavers, unable to afford power-looms, now found their product just half as valuable as before—not because their own, actual labour had changed, but because the level of socially standard labour had changed.

BEFORE THE INTRODUCTION OF THE POWER LOOM, HAND LOOM WEAVERS WENT AROUND WITH £5 NOTES STUCK IN THEIR HATBANDS.

AFTERWARDS THEY WENT ROUND 'WITH HATS...

So it should be very clear that 'equal' labour is not *real, material* labour, but real labour regarded as *socially abstract* labour.

7. ALIENATION OF USEFUL LABOUR

If, as we have said, every commodity 'contains' or 'embodies' abstract LABOUR—where is it to be found? Take a coat, for example. Is the abstract LABOUR in the lining, in the sleeves, in the collar? No. No matter how threadbare and ragged this coat may become, the abstract LABOUR it contains can never be materially found.

SO FAR, NO CHEMIST HAS EVER DISCOVERED VALUE IN A WATCH, A COAT, OR ANY OTHER COMMODITY. LOOK AT THE WATCH UNDER A MICROSCOPE! THROUGH A TELESCOPE! TURN IT UPSIDE DOWN, INSIDE OUT, EXAMINE IT AS YOU WILL — NO MATTER WHAT YOU DO, YOU WILL NEVER SEE, HEAR, TOUCH OR TASTE VALUE. ALL YOU WILL ACTUALLY SEE IS THE THING ITSELF — IN THIS CASE, THE WATCH. AND YOU WILL NEVER SEE OR HEAR AN ACTUAL LIVING PERSON ENGAGED IN ABSTRACT LABOUR.

Only useful things and useful labour can be discerned by the senses. *Since value is not material, it cannot be materially perceived.* It is social, a ghostly social reality. "The value of commodities is the very opposite of the coarse materiality of their bodies, not an atom of matter enters into it."

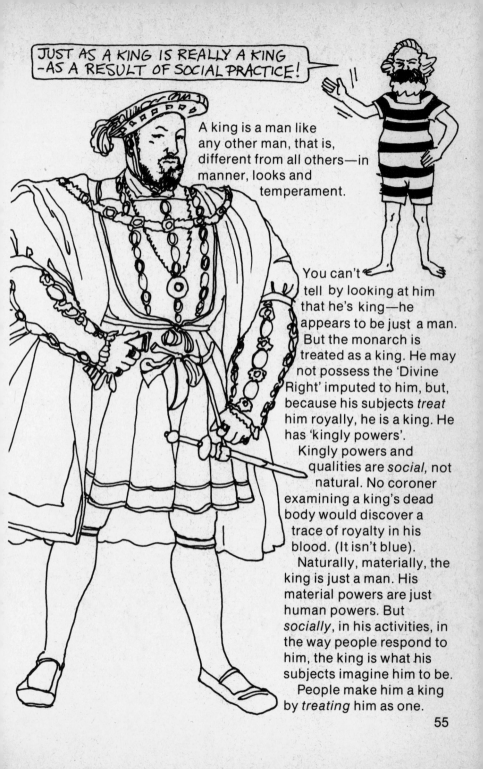

JUST AS A KING IS REALLY A KING —AS A RESULT OF SOCIAL PRACTICE!

A king is a man like any other man, that is, different from all others—in manner, looks and temperament.

You can't tell by looking at him that he's king—he appears to be just a man. But the monarch is treated as a king. He may not possess the 'Divine Right' imputed to him, but, because his subjects *treat* him royally, he is a king. He has 'kingly powers'.

Kingly powers and qualities are *social*, not natural. No coroner examining a king's dead body would discover a trace of royalty in his blood. (It isn't blue).

Naturally, materially, the king is just a man. His material powers are just human powers. But *socially*, in his activities, in the way people respond to him, the king is what his subjects imagine him to be.

People make him a king by *treating* him as one.

So it is with value. No useful object materially embodies abstract LABOUR.

A useful object can be a commodity—an embodiment of value—only be being *treated* as a commodity. But if it is treated as a commodity, then it *becomes* a commodity—*socially*.

YOU CANNOT TELL BY LOOKING AT A DIAMOND THAT IT IS A COMMODITY. WHERE IT SERVES AS AN AESTHETIC OR MECHANICAL USE-VALUE, ON THE BREAST OF A COURTESAN OR IN THE HAND OF A GLASS-CUTTER, IT IS A DIAMOND, AND NOT A COMMODITY.

In nature, there are no commodities. Just try to find value in Davy Jones' locker, or at the centre of the earth, or in outer space. Indeed, nothing is 'exchangeable' where there are no people. Exchange is an act of human relations. Exchangeability is a property possible only in the context of human social relations. But though unnatural, exchangeability can exist. *People* can make useful things exchangeable—by producing for exchange.

When exchange becomes the universal, systematic principle of production—as it is in capitalist society—then exchangeability becomes a socially real attribute of products in general. 'Ghostly' value is very, very real. Try to survive in capitalist society without buying or selling things!

With minor exceptions, *everyone* in capitalist society buys and sells commodities.

8. FETISHISM

The word **fetishism** denotes the belief that particular objects—say, religious idols or gold bars—have mystical powers. A *fetish* is precisely such an object.

To the International Gold Corporation, Gold Information Office, 30 St. George St., London W1R 9FA. I'm interested in gold, please send me more information.

Name

Address

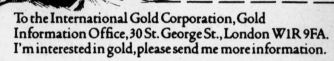

It's rare. Treasure it.

So-called primitive religions—and advanced ones, too—imagine that special entities have supernatural powers. So it is with the fetishism inherent in the world of commodities.

It seems that commodities have spontaneous, natural relations with each other...

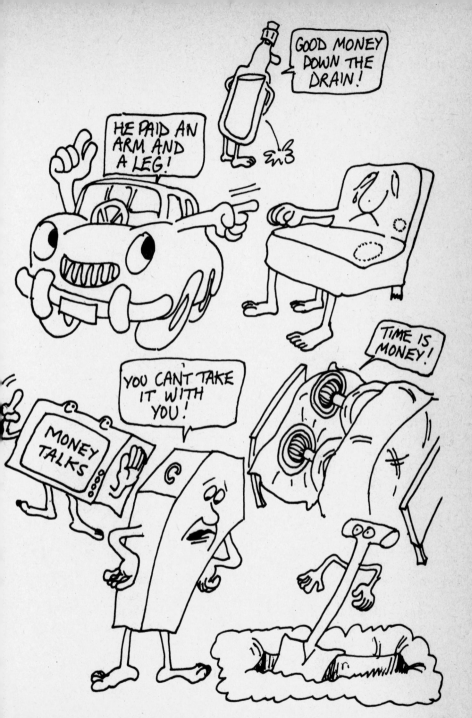

59

What really happens is that society divides its labour between a multitude of 'private producers,' who relate to each other by exchanging their products. It is this process which transforms simple use-values into magical values.

Though commodities and money do have special powers, these powers are not natural. This is, however, what people imagine. Seldom is it realised that money and commodities only have the power of exchangeability because people relate to each other as private producers. Producing in isolation from others working 'privately', producers *must* produce for exchange.

Only by exchange can products change hands. Without exchange, a private apple grower would have—only apples! To get wine, books, shoes, and other products, producers must burst from the shell of their privacy at least long enough for exchange to take place.

No one producer can use indefinite quantities of any one use-value. Beyond a certain point, the producer's product becomes a *non-use-value* for the producer, something of redeeming value only in exchange—where it appeals to some other producer as a use-value.

The appearance is that apples exchange for money (and thus, indirectly, for wine, books, and so on) *naturally*, as an expression of their inborn exchangeability. Commodities seem to attract money just as a magnet attracts iron. It seems natural for commodities to have particular prices; to be 'worth' just so much, no more and no less. This is fetishism.

— PSYCHOLOGICAL BARRIERS. PEOPLE, REARED UNDER CAPITALISM, ACQUIRE AN INGRAINED WILLINGNESS TO TAKE ORDERS, TO BOW DOWN BEFORE AUTHORITY! MANY ACQUIRE A VESTED EMOTIONAL STAKE IN ALL TYPES OF AUTHORITARIAN RELATIONS — MEN DOMINATING WOMEN, ONE NATION DOMINATING ANOTHER, ONE RACE OPPRESSING ANOTHER, HIGHER LEVELS OF THE WORKFORCE LORDING IT OVER LOWER LEVELS... AND THE MOST PROFOUND QUESTION OF REVOLUTIONARY WORKING CLASS POLITICS IS WHETHER OR NOT THESE BARRIERS CAN BE — WILL BE — OVERCOME...

— IS THAT CLEAR?

9. MONEY

Value exists in three forms: as *commodities*, *money*, and *capital*.

• COMMODITIES are use-values produced for exchange.

• MONEY is the universal commodity, equivalent to all others.

• CAPITAL is money invested to generate more money

To discuss *capital*, the very highest form of value, we must better understand money. How does money emerge from the exchange of commodities? How does money come to dominate the exchange of commodities as capital?

In the simplest case—where a single commodity is exchanged for just one equivalent commodity—the value-relation is not well established. Deciding how much 'socially average' labour is required to produce this or that is mostly a matter of guesswork. But when products are *generally* produced for exchange, value-relations grow more established. When one coat= 20 metres of linen = 10 kilos of tea = 40 kilos of coffee = 20 grammes of gold, exchange ratios become more fixed, less haphazard. Ever more products are treated as units of abstract labour. Finally, a system of commodity production arises, in which the relative value magnitudes of the different commodities are systematically fixed.

When one relative commodity is confronted not by one
equivalent commodity, but by many, its value is expressed
independently by an array of equivalents. But turn the
situation around. We can also say that each commodity in
this array of equivalents views the 'one relative' commodity
as *itself* an equivalent. If this one commodity is used to
express the value of many—it becomes *money*. It plays the
role of money most fully when it is recognised universally
as the one equivalent commodity, expressing—and
measuring—the value of all others.

GOLD

Historically, *gold* has been the particular commodity most universally used as money. With the rise of the 'gold standard', it became appropriate to say not that 1 coat = 20 metres of linen, but that 1 coat = $15 and that 20 metres of linen = $15. Coat and linen can still be exchanged, but it is now customary to use *money* to effect the trade. The equivalence of the coat and linen is expressed, not directly, but by their common relationship to gold (using one of its money-names—$, £, etc.). Gold emerges as the power of powers when it becomes the single commodity uniquely exchangeable for all others.

Coats and linen can now buy *only* money. The same is true for all ordinary commodities (with trivial exceptions).

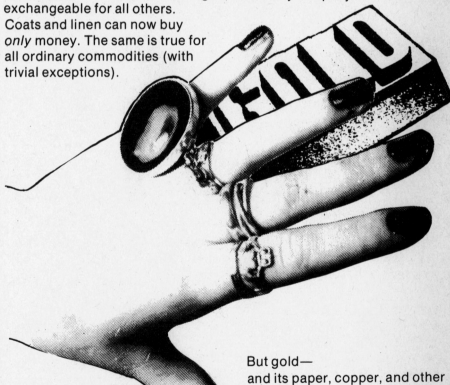

But gold—
and its paper, copper, and other representatives—can buy *any* and *every* other commodity. This is what makes it money, and sets it apart from all other commodities.

The playwright Ben Jonson conveyed a sharp sense of the real social power of money when he spoke of

RICHES – THE DUMB GOD THAT GIV'ST ALL MEN TONGUES, THAT CAN'ST DO NAUGHT, AND YET MAK'ST MEN DO ALL THINGS!

'THE ALCHEMIST'

In most early societies, gold was merely one product among others. Now, it is the one and only universal commodity, the only product that can never fail to sell. It moves faster, farther, and does more. It's ....

SUPERCOMMODITY!!

And its powers are multiplied more than ever when it functions as capital.

As capital, money does indeed 'mak'st men do all things.'

68

10. THE ACCUMULATION OF CAPITAL

WHEN WE SPEAK OF CAPITALISM, WE SPEAK NOT JUST OF MONEY, BUT OF MONEY GAIN — —OF MONEY INVESTED AS CAPITAL TO GENERATE PROFIT!

What is profit, and where does it originate? If an entrepreneur starts with a given sum of money, how does an extra sum enter his pocket? If we start with a given sum of value, where does surplus value come from?

Take our friend Lessner, a hired tailor; his father, a self-employed tailor; and Moneybags, a capitalist. Each relates to money in a different way.

Both Lessner and his father sell in order to buy. One sells the *ability* to make coats (Lessner) and the other sells coats (Lessner's father). Both seek specific, needed commodities.

The father makes and sells coats not for money as an end in itself, but as a means to obtain food, shelter, and other commodities.

> WHAT IS THE DIFFERENCE BETWEEN A WELL-DRESSED MAN AND A TIRED DOG?

The same is true for friend Lessner—he sells his ability to work not for love, but for money; for wages, as a means to obtain life's necessities.

> THE MAN WEARS AN ENTIRE SUIT, THE DOG JUST PANTS.

What we see here is the COMMODITY—MONEY—COMMODITIES cycle C-M-C, where Money is a step on the path from making Commodities to buying Commodities.

It is different with friend Moneybags. He enters the scene not as a direct producer, but as a *money-owner*. His goal is to buy commodities to sell them. He spends money to get money.

HI, PEASANTS!

THE PRODUCER NOW APPEARS AS A MAN WHO ENTERS THE MARKET, NOT WITH PRODUCE, BUT WITH MONEY; WHO BUYS NOT WHAT HE WANTS BUT WHAT HE DOES NOT WANT FOR HIS OWN USE. HE BUYS, IN A WORD, TO RESELL WHAT HE HAS BOUGHT.

ELEANOR MARX

Money, for the capitalist, is the beginning and terminus of exchange. The cycle in which Moneybags lives is the reverse of C-M-C: MONEY-COMMODITIES-MONEY (M-C-M).

73

Moneybags spends money not merely to reap an equal sum of money. He does not invest 10 merely to get 10 back.

No, Moneybags aims to get *more* money than he spends—to profit from exchange. A victim of 'the accursed hunger for gold', Moneybags finds himself on a passionate chase after value, a boundless quest for enrichment. Profit-making is his one and only goal.

HIS PERSON, OR RATHER HIS POCKET, IS THE POINT FROM WHICH THE MONEY STARTS AND TO WHICH IT RETURNS.

'More value for less'—that is the capitalist's motto.

The miracle of money is that, properly used, it does produce profit. Money makes money! An *initial* sum of money, M, gives rise to an *expanded* sum of money, M[1] (pronounced **M-prime).**

Not simply M-C-M, then, but M-C-M′ is the capitalist's cycle, where M′ is greater than M. It is here that we find the origin of *surplus value*—the difference between M′ and M. An original sum of money is replaced by an expanded sum of value. Moneybags actually achieves 'more value for less.'

Money used to generate money is 'self-expanding value', or *capital*. We speak now of the initial M. Once invested, capital gives rise to surplus value, the difference between M and M′. This surplus value takes three basic forms: **profit, interest** and **rent.**

A portion of surplus value pays the interest on M—since it is likely that Moneybags borrows at least part of the initial capital. Another portion of surplus value is used to pay rent—since it is likely that Moneybags rents at least part of the land or equipment he uses.

What remains is *profit*—surplus value belonging directly to Moneybags, to use as he pleases. There are basically two such uses: profit can be used either as *dividends*, for Moneybags' personal pleasure, or as *capital*—as a new M, to generate still further surplus value.

PRINCESS MIDIA

'AS GOOD AS GOLD'

IF WE SUBTRACT INTEREST, RENT AND DIVIDENDS FROM M' WE ARE LEFT WITH A NEW M. IF THIS M — WHICH WE CAN DESIGNATE M2 — IS GREATER THAN THE ORIGINAL M THEN CAPITAL HAS ACCUMULATED !

Though the wealth of capitalist society presents itself as an accumulation of commodities, it is, in reality, an accumulation of *capital.* Capital accumulation is the defining principle of capitalism, the economic goal and process besides which all others pale into insignificance. Capitalism is just the nickname for the system of production based on the accumulation of capital.

As we have seen, profit-making is the means by which capital accumulates. Profit keeps the system going—like wind in the sails of a boat, or uranium in a nuclear reactor.

Money has *proven* its capacity to expand
itself. Like the goose that lays the golden
egg, money has shown that it possesses the
occult power to add value to itself. Money
begets money. 'The rich get richer'.
*As capital, money tends to accumulate when invested.
Profits are made.*

Patting himself on the back, Moneybags characteristically says that profits result from 'buying cheap and selling dear', that is , *exchange.*

BUY CHEAP

—AND SELL DEAR

—PROFITS PILE UP ALL YEAR!

BUT BUY DEAR

—AND SELL CHEAP

—END UP ON THE RUBBISH HEAP!

Suppose that Moneybags sells his commodities above their value. He sells what is worth 100 for 110—thus adding a surcharge of 10. But what prevents all other sellers from doing the same? If this should happen, our friend Moneybags is at a loss—what he *gains* as a seller he *loses* as a buyer.

Swindling and shady dealing are rampant, of course. But, *in general*, overcharging for products is disallowed by competition. Rivalry between competing capitalists for limited markets and profits tends to keep prices hovering in the vicinity of value. The result is that commodities tend to sell for what they cost in terms of average, socially required labour.

Moneybags would of course like to overcharge for his products—but if he does, his competitors will cut into his sales by 'underselling' him. What Moneybags gains with his surcharge he loses in sales—if he isn't driven out of business altogether.

SURPRISING EFFECT OF COMPETITION

Consider, finally, one particular instance of swindling. Suppose that Mr A is ingenious enough to take advantage of Messrs. B and C. Fine—but will this produce surplus value? No! Some gain may occur, but this is at the expense of the gentlemen swindled. No *new* value is created.

VALUE HAS CHANGED HANDS, BUT IT HAS NOT BEEN CREATED, AND PROFITS—TO BE REAL—MUST BE NEWLY CREATED. IT IS SELF-EVIDENT THAT CAPITAL IS NOT PRODUCED BY CHEATING

ELEANOR MARX

When monopolies enter the picture, it changes somewhat—but not fundamentally. Though it *is* possible for monopolists to raise prices above values, unconstrained by competition and thus free to reap 'windfall' profits, profits, in general, are not the result of monopoly.

Without monopoly, even when production is perfectly competitive, profit is still the name of the game. The accumulation of capital started, remember, on the basis of competition. So we must look elsewhere for an explanation of profit ....

WE WORKERS DON'T SEE ANY OF THE PROFITS—

—HOWEVER BZZZY WE ARE—

—THEY HIVE THEM OFF FOR THE QUEEN —

—AND THE OTHER DRONES!

Capital is created not merely in exchange, as a *by-product* of buying and selling, but in production. *Between M and M' there is a process of production.* It is to this that we must turn if we are to grasp the origin of capital.

Q: WHAT POWER DOES MONEY HAVE?
A: JUST M-C, THE POWER TO BUY COMMODITIES.
Q: BUT M-C, WE HAVE SEEN, DOES NOT CREATE SURPLUS VALUE. WHAT DOES?
A: THE ACTION OF COMMODITIES IN PRODUCTION.
Q: EH ????!!?

More happens in M-C-M′ than exchange. Moneybags does not simply re-sell the very same commodities he buys. On the contrary, Moneybags buys commodities which give rise to new commodities.

If the value of the commodities produced is no greater than the value of the commodities purchased, Moneybags will make no profit. So Moneybags must be lucky enough to find a special commodity on the market which, once purchased, can be used to generate surplus value. As it happens, Moneybags is in luck! He does find a special, value-creating commodity on the market.

11. LABOUR-POWER

Where money is the supercommodity, human labour-power is the SUPER supercommodity. Money buying labour power for the generation of surplus value is what capitalism is all about. Only by purchasing labour power can money act as capital—and only in this way can capital be accumulated.

Capitalism ultimately depends on the commodification of labour-power. But how? By what historical process did the human capacity for labour become 'commodified'? By what process did direct producers becomes proletarians, sellers of labour-power, *workers*?

A SHORT HISTORY. A FULLER ONE COMES LATER...

PLAGUE.

PUBLICK NOTICE
YOU'VE
ALL
HADDETH
IT
by ndn

INDUSTRIAL REVOLUTION.

WAR.

GOOD LUCK
OLD CHAP!

LEISURE.

10 bn.
JOBLESS

'We know by experience that a relatively feeble development of commodity circulation suffices for the creation of money. *But* capital *requires more than the mere circulation of money and commodities. Capital arises only when the money-owner, as the owner of factories, tools, etc., finds the free worker available on the market as the seller of labour-power. This one historical precondition comprises a world's history. Capital arises on this basis, announcing a new epoch in social production.'

87

'But how are we to explain this strange phenomenon—that we find on the market a set of buyers (owning money, land, and machinery) and a set of sellers (owning nothing but labour-power, their working arms and brains)? How does it come about that one class buys continually to make profits and grow rich, while the working class continually sells its labour-power just to earn a livelihood?'

One thing is clear. Nature does not produce capitalists, on the one hand, and workers, on the other.

Social classes don't fall from the sky, or leap fully-formed from the earth. The bourgeoisie—the ruling class—and the proletariat—the working class—in particular, resulted from a long chain of historical developments.

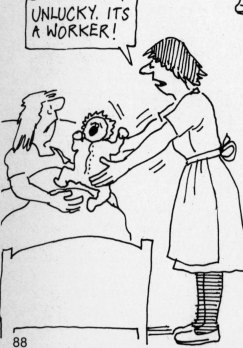

12. EXPROPRIATION

THIS PROCESS OF HISTORY
I CALL 'THE ORIGINAL
EXPROPRIATION OF THE
PRODUCER', THE SERIES
OF EVENTS AND STRUGGLES
BY WHICH PRODUCERS WERE
DIVORCED FROM THE
MEANS OF PRODUCTION.

The means of production are crucial. These
include implements, machinery, buildings,
raw materials, resources, and all other items
required for production. Production as such
is the active combination of human
energy—labour-power—and production
resources—means of production.

When production resources are
controlled by direct producers, labour-
power and means of production combine
organically. Take small farmers, growing
wheat, or artisans, making hats. Directly in
possession of the needed tools and
materials of their trades, these direct
producers simply *make use* of production
resources. The resulting production is
independent, and self-sufficient.

'But take away the land—the
livestock—the energy resources.
Wrench the tools from the
producer's hands, and what is
left? An uprooted vagabond,
whose only possession is labour-
power.'

89

This expropriation of the producer is precisely the historical precondition for capitalism. Formerly united, means of production and labour-power are now sundered. The capitalist takes possession of the means of production. Without means of production, the direct producer has nothing—except labour-power. To survive, the producer must sell his or her labour-power for wages, thus becoming a proletarian.

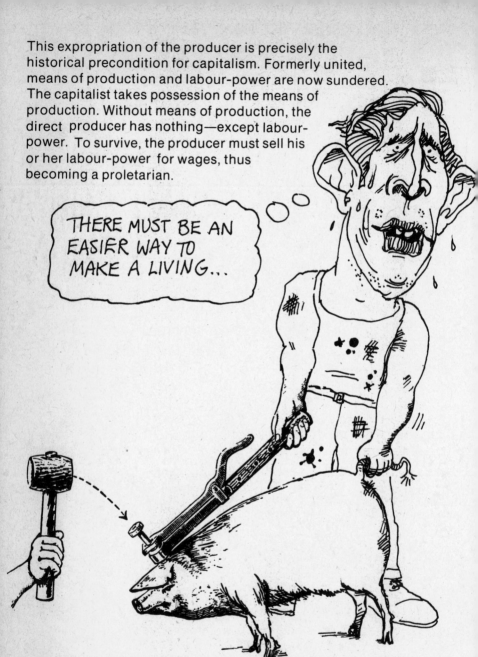

In this way, labour-power and means of production reunite—combining not organically, however, but perversely, as the playthings of a capitalist.

The proletarian finds her or himself abjectly dependent on the capitalist, for 'employment', for 'a chance to make a living', for access to means of production. Though the proletarian does all productive labour, the capitalist alone controls production—simply by owning the means of production, which allows him to buy and thus own labour-power as well.

13. A HISTORY LESSON

The historical expropriation of the direct producer took place originally in England, in the 15th, 16th and 17th centuries, and, later, throughout Europe and most of the world. In some places, this process is still going on, as producers the planet over become wage-earners.

Let's review the start of this process in England, that majestic isle, land of light and harmony where capital and the proletariat were born. It is a tale told in blood and fire ...

GO AND CAPTURE ROBIN HOOD AND BRING HIM TO JUSTICE — AAAAAARGHH!!!

SHERWOOD FOREST *

* HOME OF ROBIN HOOD. PIONEER TRADE UNION ORGANISER AND PHILANTHROPIST.

Many moralists and politicians tell an edifying story designed to enlighten us about the happy origins of wealth and poverty. 'Long, long ago,' they say, 'there were two sorts of people: one, the diligent, intelligent, and above all frugal elite; the other, lazy rascals, spending their wealth, and more, in riotous living. Thus it came to pass that the latter sort finally had nothing to sell except their own skins. And from this original sin dates the poverty of the great majority (who, despite all their labour, have up to now nothing to sell but themselves), and the wealth of the few (that increases constantly, although they long ago ceased to work).'

In real history, conquest, enslavement, robbery and murder play the greatest part. Not only the working class, but poverty, welfare, colonialism and all the rest are the result not of frail 'human nature', but of an epic assault on the common people by bosses and aristocrats of every type.

Exploitation is nothing new. By 'exploitation' we refer to the control of *surplus labour* by an armed oppressor class. Such oppressor control of surplus labour has typified every society since the introduction of slavery. It is, in fact, the hallmark of class society.

BRITAIN 1480   BRITAIN 1980s

Only its form is different in capitalist society—where *surplus labour* becomes surplus *abstract labour*, or surplus *value*.

But what, exactly, is surplus labour?

Above and beyond labour necessary for survival—
necessary labour—people may perform extra labour
resulting in surplus product—*surplus labour.* The capacity
for surplus labour is something that people acquire in
stages. At first, in the most primitive societies, labour-
power is relatively undeveloped—people are capable only
of reproducing themselves, living at bare subsistence,
picking fruits and berries, and so on. By arduous self-
development, however, people master labour skills of
greater power, like handicrafts and agriculture.

STOP WHITTLING
THAT USELESS
STICK, WOMAN—
AND COME AND
HELP ME DIG
FOR ROOTS!

WHEN ADAM DELVED
AND EVE SPAN
WHO WAS THEN THE
GENTLEMAN

When labour-power finally develops to the
point that surplus labour is possible, human
existence is revolutionised.

INDEED THE WHOLE DEVELOPMENT OF HUMAN SOCIETY BEGINS ON THE DAY WHEN THE LABOUR OF THE PRIMITIVE FAMILY CREATES MORE PRODUCTS THAN ARE NECESSARY FOR ITS MAINTENANCE. ON THE DAY WHEN THE FAMILY (SIC) DEVOTES A PORTION OF LABOUR NOT MERELY OF LIFES —

LAUNDROMAT

— NECESSITIES (MEANS OF SUBSISTENCE) BUT OF TOOLS AND MACHINES AS WELL (MEANS OF PROD- -UCTION). SURPLUS PRODUCT BECOMES THE BASIS OF ALL SOCIAL, POLITICAL, AND INTELLECTUAL PROGRESS.

FREDERICK ENGELS.

Once the earliest communal cultures had waxed and waned, surplus labour fell under the sway of a sequence of exploiting classes. In slave societies, from Greek antiquity to the 'New World', slaveowners controlled surplus labour (and necessary labour, too). In feudal cultures, serfs performed surplus labour for landlords, working several days a week on the lord's land. In each case, the cream was skimmed from the top by an armed class of owners, the slave- owners and land-owners. 'Exploitation' is nothing else but the control exercised by oppressors over the surplus labour of the oppressed.

14. THE MAKING OF THE WORKING CLASS

In capitalist society, surplus labour is extracted from the proletariat in the form of surplus value. How this came to pass we can best understand by exploring the history of the expropriation of the producer. We must cast our eyes back to that time in English history when great masses of men, women and children were suddenly and forcibly torn from their means of production and hurled onto the labour-market as sellers of labour-power. The basis of this process was the expropriation of the peasant from the land.

AS A FREE PEASANT I'VE ONLY GOT A LITTLE PIECE OF LAND

- BUT I DON'T HAVE TO WORK FOR THE BARON ANYMORE -

THE BARON

-AND IT'S BETTER THAN WORKING FOR FORD

- OR WAITING FOR THE GRUNDRISSE.

ANYWAY. I CAN'T READ.

By the end of the 14th century, English serfdom had practically disappeared. The immense majority of the population consisted of free peasants. In contrast to earlier times, these peasants did relatively little work for the nobles, working instead on land commonly or privately owned. Though gigantic baronies were strewn about, small peasant properties were much more common.

97

The violent expropriation of these small properties and proprietors occurred in several phases. Thus was formed a propertyless proletariat. The opening shot in the campaign was fired by the monarchy. In a bold move to strengthen the king against the nobles, the royal power took action to dissolve the bands of retainers surrounding the various luminaries of the nobility.

These *aides de camp* thus became the first to be hurled in appreciable numbers onto the early labour-market.

In defiant opposition, the great feudal lords created an incomparably larger proletariat, undertaking the forcible seizure of peasant land-holdings in a ruthless effort to magnify aristocratic power.

The direct impulse for this process of expropriation was provided by the rapid expansion of wool manufacture in Flanders, and the corresponding rise in wool prices. Seeking money, that emerging power of powers, the nobility decided to convert farm lands into sheepwalks.

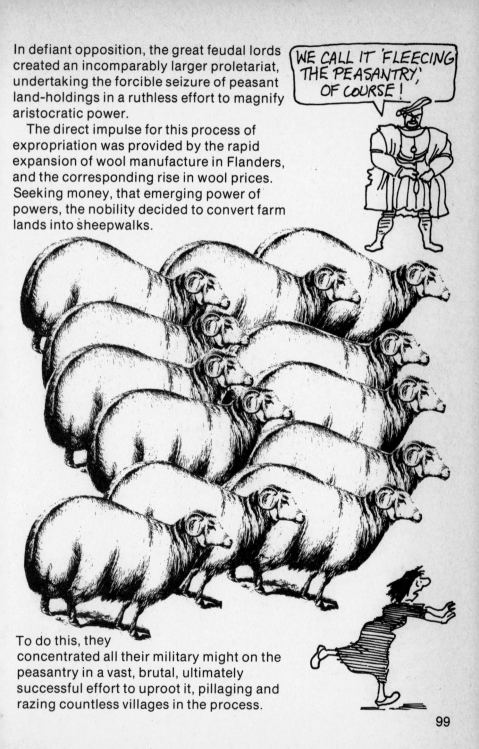

To do this, they concentrated all their military might on the peasantry in a vast, brutal, ultimately successful effort to uproot it, pillaging and razing countless villages in the process.

An Act from the time of Henry VIII speaks of the resulting transfer of control over the means of production, 'whereby many farms and large flocks of sheep became concentrated in the hands of a few men; whereby marvellous numbers of people have been deprived of the means wherewith to maintain themselves and their families.'

Henry's minister, Thomas More, speaks in Utopia of the curious land where

SHEEP SWALLOW DOWN THE VERY MEN THEMSELVES.

As Francis Bacon declared,

THIS BRED A DECAY OF PEOPLE, TOWNS, CHURCHES AND THE LIKE.

Once owners of several acres, the peasants now were virtually landless. To this day, the typical worker is lucky to own even a small garden.

The expropriation process received two new and terrible impulses during the 16th century: the theft, on a colossal scale, of Catholic Church lands (during the Protestant Reformation) and of State lands (during the 'Glorious Revolution' of 1688).

The overall result was that by methods of ruthless terrorism the lands of England were converted from community property and small holdings into a set of gigantic private business ventures. Meanwhile the number of uprooted, propertyless, and rightless ex-peasants swelled beyond measure.

101

Where did these peasants go?

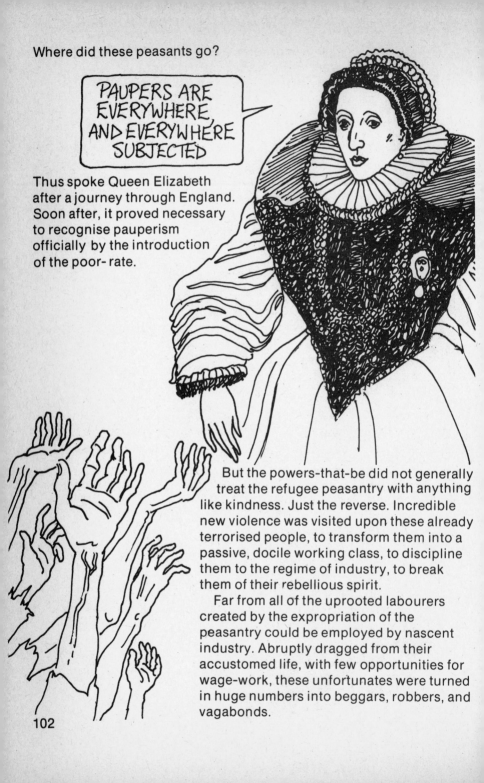

PAUPERS ARE
EVERYWHERE,
AND EVERYWHERE
SUBJECTED

Thus spoke Queen Elizabeth
after a journey through England.
Soon after, it proved necessary
to recognise pauperism
officially by the introduction
of the poor-rate.

But the powers-that-be did not generally
treat the refugee peasantry with anything
like kindness. Just the reverse. Incredible
new violence was visited upon these already
terrorised people, to transform them into a
passive, docile working class, to discipline
them to the regime of industry, to break
them of their rebellious spirit.

Far from all of the uprooted labourers
created by the expropriation of the
peasantry could be employed by nascent
industry. Abruptly dragged from their
accustomed life, with few opportunities for
wage-work, these unfortunates were turned
in huge numbers into beggars, robbers, and
vagabonds.

102

The State promptly showed its great and tender regard for the newly impoverished by enacting Draconian laws treating beggars and vagabonds as 'voluntary criminals.

• During the reign of Henry VIII, in 1530, vagabonds were condemned to whipping for a first offence, loss of an ear for a second, and execution for a third—with no help offered in finding work.

• During the reign of Edward VI, in 1547, anyone refusing to work—at what? with what means of production?—was condemned as a slave.

• During the reign of Elizabeth, in 1572, unlicensed beggars 14 or older were severely flogged and branded. A second offence brought death.

'Thus were the farming folk of England expropriated, chased from their homes, turned into vagabonds, and then whipped, branded, and tortured by grotesquely terroristic laws into accepting the discipline necessary for the system of wage labour.'

103

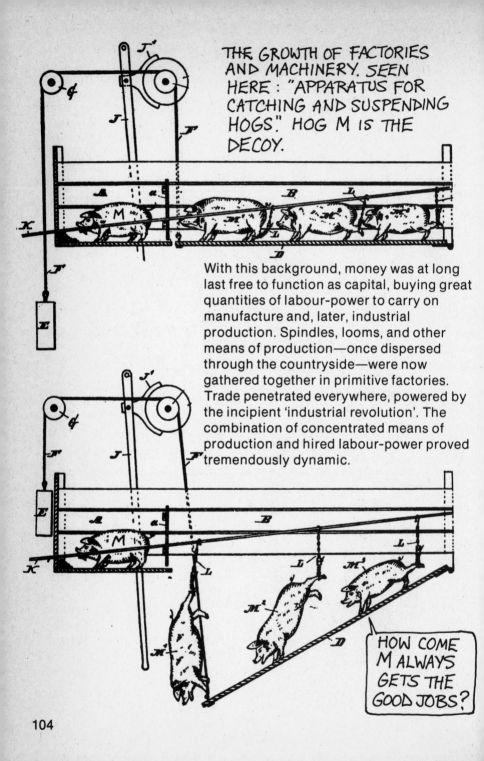

THE GROWTH OF FACTORIES AND MACHINERY. SEEN HERE: "APPARATUS FOR CATCHING AND SUSPENDING HOGS." HOG M IS THE DECOY.

With this background, money was at long last free to function as capital, buying great quantities of labour-power to carry on manufacture and, later, industrial production. Spindles, looms, and other means of production—once dispersed through the countryside—were now gathered together in primitive factories. Trade penetrated everywhere, powered by the incipient 'industrial revolution'. The combination of concentrated means of production and hired labour-power proved tremendously dynamic.

HOW COME M ALWAYS GETS THE GOOD JOBS?

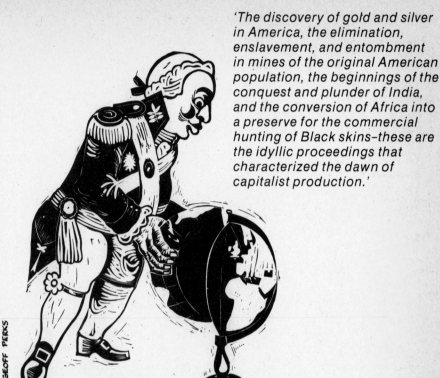

'The discovery of gold and silver in America, the elimination, enslavement, and entombment in mines of the original American population, the beginnings of the conquest and plunder of India, and the conversion of Africa into a preserve for the commercial hunting of Black skins–these are the idyllic proceedings that characterized the dawn of capitalist production.'

GEOFF PERKS

JOHN BULL SAILED AROUND THE WORLD
TO LOOK FOR LAND TO SEIZE –
HE STOLE SOME ISLANDS IN THE WEST
AND CALLED THEM HIS WEST INDIES

At first, capital could absorb a mere fraction of the surplus population driven from the land, leaving beggars and vagbonds unemployed in droves. But, once underway, capitalist production gathered momentum. As decades and centuries passed, the immense majority of the English population became proletarians. The same happened elsewhere, too.

The terroristic methods and harsh laws by which the landless population had initially been introduced to labour discipline became decreasingly necessary as capitalist production stabilised, becoming the 'normal' form of production.

CLOCK HERE

'Now, the silent compulsion of economic relations sets the seal on the domination of the capitalist over the worker. Direct extra-economic force is still of course used, but only in exceptional cases. In the ordinary run of things, workers can safely be left to the gentle mercy of production relations–to fears of joblessness, to hunger and need...'

Because they possess no means of production, workers have no option but to 'freely' sell their labour-power. It is in this way that the proletariat becomes the principal actor on the economic stage.

'SOME EXHIBITS WHICH WILL NOT BE ON SHOW AT THE GREAT EXHIBITION'. PUNCH, 1851.

The proletariat differs from openly unfree classes like serfs and slaves in two ways. Proletarians are 'free' to sell labour-power, and (unlike serfs) 'free' of all means of production. This is the double basis of the celebrated 'freedom' of bourgeois society.

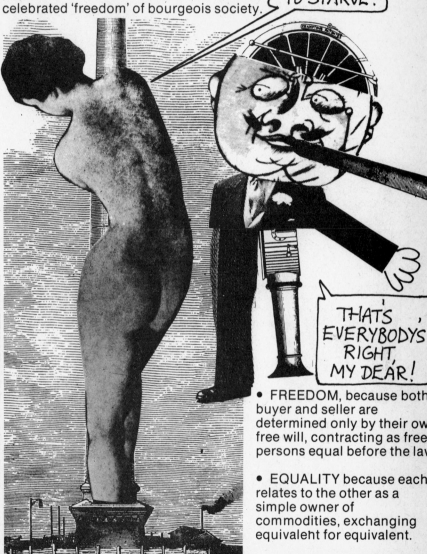

FREEDOM TO STARVE?

THAT'S EVERYBODY'S RIGHT, MY DEAR!

• FREEDOM, because both buyer and seller are determined only by their own free will, contracting as free persons equal before the law.

• EQUALITY because each relates to the other as a simple owner of commodities, exchanging equivalent for equivalent.

• PROPERTY, because each disposes only of what is his own.

107

But when we leave the sphere of exchange—when we enter the hidden abode of *production,* on whose threshold hangs the notice, 'No admittance expect on business'—a certain change takes place in the manner of our leading characters.

The money-owner now strides forward as a capitalist; the possessor of labour-power follows as his worker. The one smirks self-importantly and is intent on business; the other is deferential and fearful. We are now speaking about the *alienation of labour*—the subordination of the worker to an alien power. As the direct outcome of the sale of labour-power, the subordination of the worker is an intrinsic feature of labour-power's status as a commodity. Comprising a false freedom—the 'freedom' to enter a subservient role—labour's alienation is the vital prerequisite for its exploitation.

The worker's freedom is a curious matter. It should be evident, on balance, that the worker, as a participant in commodity exchange, is free to do just one thing: sell time and energy for wages. Different bosses and different jobs are available but workers can avoid bosses and jobs only if they don't care about 'making a living'. Everyone knows that there are just two kinds of workers: employed and unemployed.

With the sale of labour-power, working people lose all control over what they do. What is produced and how—the purposes and methods of labour—are questions only the capitalist may answer. And the *result* of labour—the product itself—unquestionably belongs not to the producer but to the capitalist.

An alien will, concerned not about the worker but about profit, decides what the worker does. The motives of working people are entirely discounted in production, trampled by the profit-motive.

Moneybags sternly warns the worker:

JUST DO WHAT YOU'RE TOLD! THAT'S WHAT YOU'RE HERE FOR — YOU'RE NOT PAID TO THINK! WHAT YOU DO ON YOUR OWN TIME IS YOUR OWN AFFAIR, BUT HERE YOU DO WHAT I SAY. WHAT YOU PRODUCE IS NONE OF YOUR BUSINESS. IF YOU DON'T LIKE MAKING NERVE GAS, OR NEUTRON BOMBS OR DEFECTIVE CARS OR ADULTERATED FOODS, YOU CAN LOOK FOR WORK ELSEWHERE. DO I MAKE MYSELF CLEAR?

Workers are never allowed any say about what to produce, or why. 'Investment decisions'— *how* and *why* to employ labour-power and means of production, say, whether to make nuclear weapons or candy—are the prerogative of capital.

110

By selling labour-power—a matter of 'free choice' in name only—the worker surrenders control over labour. In this way labour, the *use* of labour-power, is *alienated,* just as the use of commodities is alienated in general. The difference is that labour, once sold, can never be recovered.

Bread, though its usefulness is repressed while it awaits sale,can at least be eaten when it does sell. The use of labour-power, by contrast, is most fully alienated *after* its sale.

Though working people may resist the tyranny of the capitalist in various way, this is done at personal risk. Workers can be fired. The capitalist can refuse to continue buying labour-power. At this point, the worker is severed both from *means of production* and *means of subsistence.* Though resistance, to be sure, is possible and necessary it doesn't alter the basic fact: that being a worker means being dependent on the capitalist.

And Moneybags has the law on his side. After all, he buys your labour-power, doesn't he? So it's his—to use as he likes. If you object, just ask the police—or the courts. You'll learn quickly enough that the use of labour-power belongs to its rightful, legal owner—Moneybags.

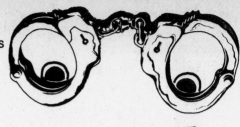

POLICE FIRE ON STRIKERS: U.S. 1932

15. SURPLUS VALUE

ACCUMULATE! ACCUMULATE! THAT IS MOSES AND THE PROPHETS TO THE CAPITALIST!

CAPITAL

Alienation of labour is the fundamental prerequisite for its exploitation. Sold to be used, labour-power must be *alienated* to be *exploited*. It then becomes the source of surplus value.

Overcharging for commodities does *not* create surplus value; exploiting the working class *does.*

How so?

People have had the capacity to perform surplus labour for millennia, ever since the first revolution in agriculture. In contemporary, capitalist society, the primary result of surplus labour is *surplus value*. Remember M-C-M′? Capital seeks to expand—to multiply—to embody more abstract labour after investment than before.

113

KEEP TAKING THE TABLETS!

CAPITAL

Moneybags wants to buy ever more labour-power, ever more means of production. To do this, ever more money is needed. This expanding stock of money is supplied by the exploitation of the worker.

THOUGH MARX HAD MANY WORTHY ANTECEDENTS – PETTY, BOISGUILLEBERT, FRANKLIN, GALIANI, STEUART, QUESNAY, RICARDO – IT WAS MARX'S INSIGHT THAT LED TO THE EXPLANATION OF SURPLUS VALUE. WHAT MARX DISCOVERED IS THAT THE VALUE OF LABOUR-POWER MAY BE LESS THAN THE VALUE OF THE LABOUR PRODUCT. THIS IS THE SECRET OF SURPLUS VALUE, AT LAST REVEALED.

What is the value of a commodity? Just this: the average, socially required labour-time necessary to make it. Since labour-power in capitalist society is also a commodity, it too, has a value. This is the average labour-time required to 'produce' the worker; to keep the worker alive and productive ... just what it costs to replenish the worker's energy, so that *tomorrow's* labour-power will be roughly the same as *today's*.

Historically, the work of reproducing labour-power has been reserved for women, as wives and mothers...

The signal fact is that workers are capable of producing commodities more valuable than labour-power itself.

8 HOURS FOR OUR OWN INSTRUCTION AND 8 HOURS FOR REPOSE • WE REQUIRE 8 HOURS FOR WORK •

The value of the labour product may exceed the value of labour-power—that is, the average labour-time socially required to keep a worker going may be less than the average, socially required labour-time the worker expends making commodities. Paying the worker for the value of his or her labour-power ordinarily requires less money than the capitalist gets in return for the product the worker produces.

Take any worker, at random. If $50 is the cost of supplying the worker with means of subsistence, a capitalist is foolhardy to pay this unless the worker's product (say, bread) turns out to be worth *more* than $50. Otherwise, the capitalist will go out of business. But if the worker does produce commodities worth more than the initial investment, all is well. The investment 'works': money is 'made'.

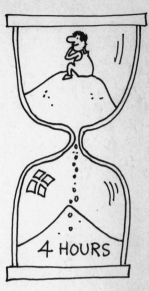

TIME IT TAKES FOR THE WORKER TO PROVIDE FOR HIMSELF.

4 HOURS

If it happens that the worker produces commodities equal in value to the worker's labour-power in just *part* of a workday—say, in 4 hours—there is nothing to prevent the capitalist from employing the worker for *more* than 4 hours—say, 8 hours. When this does, in fact, happen (as it regularly does!), *surplus value* is the result.

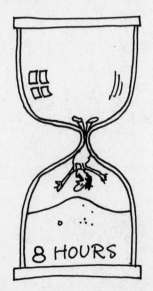

8 HOURS

TIME IT TAKES WHEN SURPLUS LABOUR IS ADDED ON.

The 4 hours necessary to produce commodities as valuable as the worker's labour-power we call (surprise!)— NECESSARY LABOUR. The *extra* time spent producing commodities we call SURPLUS LABOUR. Assuming that the worker spends roughly the average labour-time socially required to produce whatever is produced, this labour counts as so much abstract, socially equal labour-value. The surplus accumulated is surplus abstract labour—*surplus value.*

117

IF THE WORKER'S LABOUR IS SUB-AVERAGE, IT MAY STILL PRODUCE SURPLUS VALUE–BUT LESS. IT COUNTS AS LESS ABSTRACT LABOUR THAN IT WOULD HAVE IF IT HAD BEEN AT LEAST AVERAGE. FOR EXAMPLE: 8 HOURS OF LESS-THAN AVERAGE LABOUR MIGHT RESULT IN THE PRODUCTION OF COMMODITIES NORMALLY REQUIRING ONLY 6 HOURS TO PRODUCE. IT WOULD THUS COUNT AS ONLY 6 HOURS OF ABSTRACT LABOUR –BUT IF NECESSARY LABOUR REQUIRES ONLY 4 LABOUR HOURS THERE IS STILL A SURPLUS OF TWO. THIS IS ONLY HALF AS MUCH SURPLUS AS AVERAGE, BUT IT IS A SURPLUS. ON THE OTHER HAND, IF THE WORKER'S LABOUR IS SO SUB-AVERAGE THAT THE WORKER FAILS TO PRODUCE COMMODITIES OF ENOUGH VALUE TO COMPENSATE FOR PAYMENT OF WAGES THEN THE BOSS WILL GO BANKRUPT.

REASONABLE 'AVERAGE' MANAGEMENT

MONEYBAGS BUYS TWO TYPES OF COMMODITIES TO SET THE PRODUCTION PROCESS IN MOTION. OUR OLD FRIENDS LABOUR POWER AND MEANS OF PRODUCTION! MONEY THUS FUNCTION AS CAPITAL IN TWO PRINCIPAL WAYS: 1. BUYING LIVING HUMAN ENERGY, AND, 2. BUYING PRODUCTION RESOURCES THE PRODUCT, IN PART, OF PREVIOUS HUMAN ENERGY!

Das Kapital

VARIABLE CAPITAL

This gives us our criterion for distinguishing different forms of capital. Since the value added to the commodity by labour-power *varies,* introducing the possibility of a surplus, we call the money spent for labour-power VARIABLE CAPITAL.

CONSTANT CAPITAL

Since the value contributed in production by means of production does *not* vary, we call money spent for means of production CONSTANT CAPITAL.

THAT'S US !

VARIABLE CAPITAL

AND

CONSTANT CAPITAL

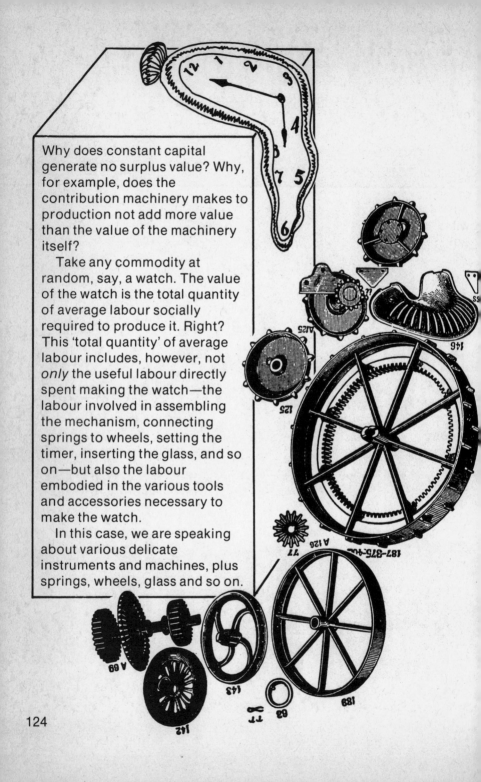

Why does constant capital generate no surplus value? Why, for example, does the contribution machinery makes to production not add more value than the value of the machinery itself?

Take any commodity at random, say, a watch. The value of the watch is the total quantity of average labour socially required to produce it. Right? This 'total quantity' of average labour includes, however, not *only* the useful labour directly spent making the watch—the labour involved in assembling the mechanism, connecting springs to wheels, setting the timer, inserting the glass, and so on—but also the labour embodied in the various tools and accessories necessary to make the watch.

In this case, we are speaking about various delicate instruments and machines, plus springs, wheels, glass and so on.

Moneybags buys these tools and accessory products so that a hired watchmaker can use them to make a watch.

In general, we assume that Moneybags buys this watch-making equipment for what it's worth—that is, an exchange of equivalents takes place, in which Moneybags pays as much for the equipment as the equipment is actually worth in terms of the abstract labour it contains.

If this happens, *no surplus value* will be created by the use of this equipment. Why not? Here's why:

EXPLANATION

Imagine, for a moment, that Moneybags purchases just enough watchmaking equipment (machinery and materials) to produce 100 watches. By the time these watches are completed, every machine will be used up and every accessory product will be used.

THIS MACHINE I'VE MADE MAKES 100 WATCHES BY ITSELF. BUT WHEN IT'S MADE THEM—

Assume further that the total value of this equipment is $1,000 —just what Moneybags pays for it. Now, if the total value of the watches is the quantity of average labour socially required to produce them, how much value will the watchmaking equipment add to these watches? *Just as much abstract labour as this equipment actually contains*—no more, and no less. Moneybags has paid for a specific sum of abstract labour— and this abstract labour then goes into the product Moneybags sponsors.

IT'S WORN OUT. MONEYBAGS NEEDS **ME** TO MEND IT —TO GENERATE NEW SURPLUS VALUE!

TOO BAD. I'M OFF TO THE PUB TO FINISH READING THE— GRUNDRISSE!

The total value of the watches is the sum of *two* elements:

the number of average labour
hours expended in producing
the equipment,

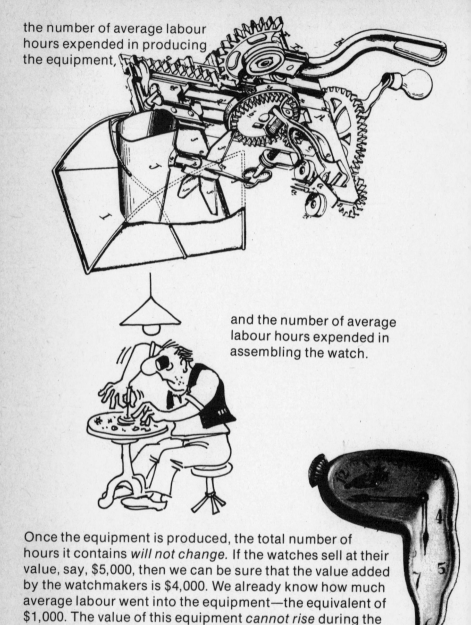

and the number of average
labour hours expended in
assembling the watch.

Once the equipment is produced, the total number of
hours it contains *will not change.* If the watches sell at their
value, say, $5,000, then we can be sure that the value added
by the watchmakers is $4,000. We already know how much
average labour went into the equipment—the equivalent of
$1,000. The value of this equipment *cannot rise* during the
production process; we can't pretend that more average
labour goes into this equipment than actually does.

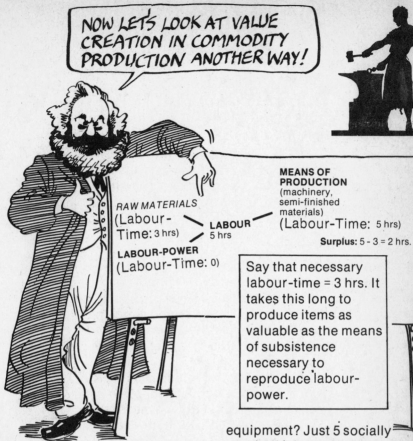

NOW LET'S LOOK AT VALUE CREATION IN COMMODITY PRODUCTION ANOTHER WAY!

RAW MATERIALS
(Labour-Time: 3 hrs)

LABOUR-POWER
(Labour-Time: 0)

LABOUR
5 hrs

MEANS OF PRODUCTION
(machinery, semi-finished materials)
(Labour-Time: 5 hrs)

Surplus: 5 - 3 = 2 hrs.

Say that necessary labour-time = 3 hrs. It takes this long to produce items as valuable as the means of subsistence necessary to reproduce labour-power.

Set labour-power to work with no special equipment — just raw materials and skill — to produce means of production, i.e., the machinery and semi-finished materials necessary to make watches. Assume that zero socially required labour-time is embodied in the raw materials. If it now takes 5 hours of socially required labour to transform these genuinely 'raw' materials into watchmaking machinery and semi-finished materials —what is the value of this watchmaking equipment? Just 5 socially required labour-hours:

zero labour hours to produce raw materials
+
five to transform raw materials into equipment.

since 3 labour-hours are socially required to reproduce power, surplus labour here = 2 hours: the difference between the time socially required for watchmaking equipment (5 average hours) and the time required for labour-power (3 average labour-hours).

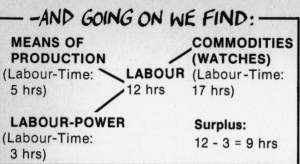

—AND GOING ON WE FIND:—

**MEANS OF
PRODUCTION**
(Labour-Time:
5 hrs)

LABOUR
12 hrs

**COMMODITIES
(WATCHES)**
(Labour-Time:
17 hrs)

LABOUR-POWER
(Labour-Time:
3 hrs)

Surplus:
12 - 3 = 9 hrs

If it requires *5 hours* to produce watch-making equipment, and then *12 hours* to use up this equipment making watches, what quantity of total, socially required labour-time goes into these watches?

That's simple arithmetic: 5 + 12 = 17. Exactly 17 labour-hours are required to produce and use means of production for the production of watches for sale. All socially required labour-power is now present and accounted for. But how much surplus value is generated in this watchmaking process?

If necessary labour-time — the value of labour-power – equals 3 average labour-hours, and total labour-time - the value of the labour product – equals 12 average hours, the difference is surplus value: 12 - 3 + 9. Assuming that the watchmakers receive the equivalent (in wages) of 3 labour-hours, Moneybags thus accrues the equivalent (in money) of 9 labour-hours. That's surplus value.

Do the means of production add to this surplus value? No! The total value of the product unquestionably includes the labour-time socially required to produce means of production. As we've seen, the total value of the watches = 17 labour-hours: 12 using means of production plus 5 making means of production. But surplus value results only from the difference between the value created and the value presupposed — and only labour-power creates more value than it presupposes. Means of production, used up in production, add just the value they contain; in this case, 5 labour-hours.

To be sure, production of means of production may generate surplus value. (Indeed, as we saw earlier, if it takes 5 labour-hours to produce watchmaking equipment but only 3 labour-hours to reproduce labour-power, surplus value does accrue.) But again: this surplus value is created by the exercise of labour-power, which thus shows itself capable of creating products more valuable than itself (by a ratio of 5:3, in this case).

16. THE RATE OF SURPLUS VALUE

In M–C–M′, the basic change is from M to M[1]. We can now show this by two new equations:

1. Capital = constant capital + variable capital, or Capital = c + v.

2. Capital′ = constant capital + variable capital + *surplus value,* or Capital′ = c + v + s.

c = constant capital
v = variable capital
s = surplus value

I TRY TO KEEP THIS **DOWN**–

The difference between Capital—Capital′ (or between M–M′, if this is how we choose to depict it) is *surplus value,* s.

Since v is the source of s, it makes sense to compare s and v. Surplus value/variable capital is the *rate of surplus value.* When v = 5 and s = 5, s/v = 1—in other words, this represents an exactly 100% rate of surplus value.

THE RATE OF PROFIT

–AND I TRY TO KEEP THIS **UP**!

The RATE OF PROFIT is the ratio between s and total investment, both constant *and* variable capital—that is, s/v+c, or s/Capital.

Whenever c is greater than zero, the rate of profit is less than the rate of surplus value. **This is very important.** Why? Because it helps to explain why there is a tendency for the rate of profit to *fall;* why capitalism tends to profit-crunches; why, in a word, economic crisis is such a basic part of life in capitalist society.

When *c rises* there tend to be *crises!*

The ratio of constant to variable capital we
call the ORGANIC COMPOSITION OF
CAPITAL. When c rises relative to v, we say
that the organic composition of capital
rises. In other words, the more means of
production are employed relative to labour-
power, the higher is the organic
composition of capital.

HIGH ORGANIC COMPOSITION OF CAPITAL.

LOW ORGANIC COMPOSITION OF CAPITAL.

As everyone knows, capital production tends to rely ever
more on increasingly powerful means of production. Every
day, high technology gets higher—more powerful
machines enter production, and productivity soars. From
simple hand tools-spindles, looms, hammers, anvils-
production advances to nuclear power plants, automated
factories, advanced computer systems, and much, much
more.

130

Historically, the most important reason for the rapid growth of capitalist-owned means of production is *competition*. When Moneybags decides to buy labour-power and means of production to produce watches, he embarks on a risky venture. There are other firms making watches, and a less-than-infinite market. Who can sell watches? How many can be sold? For what price?

If Moneybags is fortunate, he, rather than his competitors, will get a large share of the market. To do this, though, Moneybags needs to sell his products as cheaply as possible. Unless he is willing to sell products for less than they are worth (which sometimes happens, but as an exception, not the rule), this means that he must cut the average labour-time socially required for the production of watches. If it originally requires 20 hours of average labour-time to make a watch, Moneybags must find some way to produce a watch in *less* than 20 hours.

When he does, he can then charge less for his product with no loss in surplus value, and win a higher percentage of the market. If his competitor, Cashbox, finds a way to cut prices by cutting labour-time, Moneybags must follow suit—or go out of business when Cashbox 'corners the market'.

To make a long, unlovely story shorter and sweeter, the point is that competition forces capital to use ever less labour-time per commodity. First, Moneybags cuts the time required to produce a watch from 20 hours to 18. Then Cashbox retaliates by cutting it still further. And so it goes, like a tug of war. Cutting prices, as we will see, is a way to cut throats—to eliminate competitors.

 HOW IS AVERAGE LABOUR-TIME REDUCED?

EASY, FRED! BY INCREASING THE POWER OF THE MEANS OF PRODUCTION! THE TIME SPENT PRODUCING A TOOL IS GENERALLY FAR LESS THAN THE TIME THE TOOL SAVES. OTHERWISE, WHY PRODUCE IT?

EVEN IF THE INSTRUMENT ITSELF REQUIRES PRODIGIOUS TIME AND ENERGY—SAY AN OIL REFINERY—THE TIME AND ENERGY IT SAVES IS EVEN MORE PRODIGIOUS. IF IT TAKES 70 EXTRA HOURS TO MAKE AN ELECTRIC TYPEWRITER SELF-CORRECTING, THE TIME THIS SAVES LATER IN CORRECTING ERRORS ON TENS OF THOUSANDS OF PAGES WILL BE ENORMOUS!

 (YOUR AUTHOR) NO KIDDING!

And this is even more true for more powerful instruments.

The golden rule of competitive profit-making is to produce *more* for *less*—to cut costs by cutting the average labour-time required for production. How? By increasing the power of the means of production.

IN STALIN'S RUSSIA IN THE 1930's ALEXEI STAKHANOV, A MINER (RT), VASTLY EXCEEDED NORMAL OUTPUT. STALIN SENT HIM ROUND THE COUNTRY TO PREACH 'STAKHANOVISM'.

BUT THE OTHER WORKERS SAID:

IF STAKHANOV IS SO KEEN—

—LET **HIM** DO ALL THE WORK!

It's a simple rule—but one with earthshaking consequences. Productivity, revolutionised, rises steeply. The world fills with commodities, and the danger of economic crisis approaches.

What's the connection? Just this: *that s derives from v. Variable capital, not constant capital,* produces surplus value. If competition forces capital to employ an ever higher ratio of constant to variable capital—as it clearly does—then the rate of profit (s/v+c) tends to fall.

When more is spent on means of production relative to labour-power, the rate of profit tends to decline. Say, for example, that initially c = 16, v = 8, and s = 8 (so that a 100% rate of surplus value, s/v, obtains). If c rises with no corresponding rise in v and s, the rate of profit grows smaller (even though the rate of surplus value does not). Say c changes to c = *24. Then s/v+c changes from (8/8+16 = 1/3) to 8/8+24 = 1/4).*

From the standpoint of the capitalist, this is a big and appalling drop.

A RAILWAY MEETING : EMOTION OF THE SHAREHOLDERS AT THE ANNOUNCEMENT OF A DIVIDEND OF 2½D.

Producing for exchange is risky—it's possible that the product will fail to sell, either as a result of competition or for other reasons.

To make the gamble of investment worthwhile requires a certain minimum prospect of gain. If the rate of profit falls too low, investment ceases to be a wise use of money—the risk of loss is too great, the potential for gain is too slight.

This is all the more true when investment becomes, typically, a matter of ever increasing billions of dollars—a tendency which parallels the tendency of the organic composition of capital to rise, and the tendency of the rate of profit to fall.

This is not just hypothetical. That the rate of profit has a tendency to fall is borne out by myriad facts of economic history. This tendency is not, however, *absolute.* There are *countertendencies* as well. But who can fail to notice the profit squeeze now stalking the world?

SPEAKING HISTORICALLY WE KNOW THAT 'C' RISES FASTER THAN 'V'. EVERY YEAR MORE MEANS OF PRODUCTION ARE EMPLOYED PER UNIT OF LABOUR-POWER. THOUGH THE TOTAL NUMBER OF WORKERS RISES TOO, THE WORLD OVER, THIS HAPPENS AT A SLOWER PACE THAN THE RATE AT WHICH THE TOTAL MASS OF MEANS OF PRODUCTION GROWS. IN GENERAL, AS A RESULT, S/V+C DECLINES OVER TIME. THE RATE OF PROFIT FALLS.

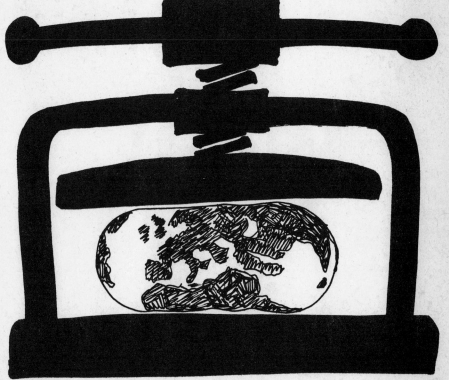

Previous profit squeezes have led to trade wars, often culminating in shooting wars. For competition leads not just to *cutthroat business*—Moneybags and Cashbox battling over price and markets—but to the *business of cutting throats.*

War is the ultimate means of securing economic advantage, letting your competitors suffer whatever losses must be incurred while you seize resources and markets directly without recourse to the genteel etiquette of exchange. For the victor, it is an excellent means of evading a fall in profits.

M—C—M

$E = MC^2$

WAR!

ALSO LATE FOOTBALL RESULTS

Some of the countertendencies to the tendency for the rate of profit to fall are vastly important, not only as such, but in their own right. These countertendencies revolve around v (variable capital) and s (surplus value). If c rises, what can maintain or improve the rate of profit? A comparable increase in s or a decrease in v? Let's consider these in turn.

If necessary labour is still 4 hours, and if the number of workers stays constant, then extra surplus value can be extracted by adding extra hours to the working day. A working day of 8 hours will yield 4 hours. of unpaid surplus labour-time— but a working day of 10 hours will yield 6, and a working day of 12 hours will *double* the original surplus value. With no change in v—neither the value of the labour-power nor the total number of workers changes—*s rises.*

This we call the extraction of ABSOLUTE SURPLUS VALUE.

By compelling the worker to work longer hours, Moneybags forces an absolute increase in surplus value. This is pure, unbridled joy for the capitalist, the pleasure of getting something for nothing. For the worker, the compulsory performance of absolutely more surplus labour is something else entirely—a journey through purgatory, into the hell of overwork.

Is it accidental that the antagonistic relations between capital and labour so constantly revolve around the length of the working day? No! Starting with legal enactments in the 14th century, capital has fought long and hard to keep the worker *at work* as much as possible.

A MOUNTAIN OF BILLIARD BALLS — THE TUSKS OF 2,000 ELEPHANTS

In the brutal glory days of early English capitalism, when capital was organised but labour wasn't, horror stories abounded. Countless thousands of children of between 7 and 12 were literally worked to death— forced to work from before sunrise to midnight or later. Capital's voracious, vampire appetite for labour brought death to innumerable workers.

FORGET CHILDREN—I'M INTERESTED IN ELEPHANTS!

Even in the unusual event that restrictions were imposed at all, it remained legal and 'respectable' to keep small children at work from 5.30 a.m. to 8.00 p.m. The majority of the time, there were no restrictions at all — just the ceaseless torment of hard, hot, dangerous work in lightless, chokingly dirty factories and mines.

Children, women and men perished by the multitude, after brutish and nasty lives shortened by overwork. Penniless even when employed, workers in these 'dark satanic mills' (so-called by the visionary poet William Blake) were crippled and maimed in untold ways and numbers. Family life was totally disrupted, with fathers, mothers, and children chained to machines...

141

The only power serving to limit capital's effort to turn every waking hour into a working hour was the proletariat itself. By means of bitter struggles against unequal, seemingly impossible odds, against greedy and complacent foes defended by the armed might of the State, workers organised to reduce the working day to more acceptable dimensions. Intense and intricate battles ensued.

The result was that organised labour showed capital its power by shortening the working day. Moneybags and his vulture-brothers yielded with bitter resentment, forced to swallow gall and wormwood in the guise of first a 10 hour workday, and later an 8 hour day.

Capital hates and despises this misfortune, resisting the reduction of the workday with all its might—to this day seeking to subvert the workers' gains and seeking places elsewhere in the world where less organised workers may be coerced into 16 hour and 18 hour days. In many places, where the process of industrial production and the creation of the proletariat is still a recent development, capital succeeds in its quest. Just ponder Taiwan, Korea, Brazil, India, South Africa...

So the battle over *absolute surplus value* continues. S rises and falls at different times and in different parts of the world as the balance of power between capital and labour see-saws back and forth. Here labour forces absolute surplus value down—there capital forces it up.

143

Meanwhile, there are other fronts in the battle over surplus value. Say, for example, that workers are forced to work *faster*. If the value of labour-power remains unchanged, then it now requires fewer labour hours to produce commodities equal in value to the value of labour-power.

Working faster, our harassed worker produces in three hours what formerly required 4 hours to produce. Where once 4 hours comprised necessary labour-time, now 3 hours does so. Even without lengthening the working day, capital can thus extract extra surplus value. An extra hour of surplus labour is extracted—and *every* hour of surplus labour is now equal to 4/3 of one labour hour *before* the work was speeded up. If we assume that the earlier labour was socially average, the present, faster labour is *above average* in intensity, resolving itself into *more* hours of *average* labour than before.

145

Or suppose that the *value of labour-power* falls. This occurs, willy nilly, whenever the average labour-time socially required to produce the means of subsistence falls. By means of rising productivity in the food industry, the construction trades, and related industries, foodstuffs and other basic subsistence necessitities may be sold at cheaper prices.

When this happens, the value of labour-power—roughly, the cost of reproducing labour-power through the purchase of basic necessities—also falls. The result is that *fewer* hours of labour are now required to produce commodities as valuable as labour-power—since the value of labour-power has *fallen*.

By reducing that part of the workday devoted to necessary labour in either of these two ways—by speedup, or by cutting the value of labour-power—capital extracts what we call RELATIVE SURPLUS VALUE. Without *absolutely* lengthening the workday, capital nevertheless succeeds in expanding s by freeing *relatively* more of the workday for unpaid surplus labour.

Again, s rises—counteracting the tendency of the rate of profit to fall. And again, it is only the working class that can defend itself.

Speedup can be prevented from reaching a killing pace only by the action of workers organised for their own ends—as the telling lessons of sweatshop labour make clear. In countless places, Moneybags, Cashbox, and their bloodthirsty colleagues try to push labour faster, faster, and still faster—typically, by the ploy of speeding up the machines until the workers keel over. Or they turn to the ruse of 'scientific management,' bringing in 'efficiency experts' with stopwatches (*à la* Frederick Winslow Taylor) to reduce 'wasted motions' and thus generate higher productivity.

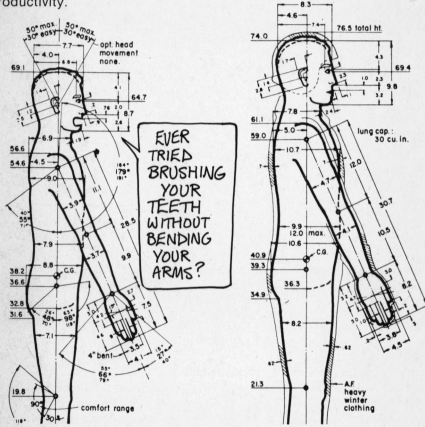

Or management psychology is used: 'What colour should we paint the factory, and what *muzak* should we play, to lull the workers into working harder?' Or direct force is employed, with the use of brutal foremen and supervisors.

In places where labour is strong, decisive steps have been taken to combat speed-up. But where labour remains weak, capital is overjoyed to speed workers as fast as it can and for as long as it can. Until labour is strong everywhere, capital will scour the earth for unorganised sectors of the world proletariat to exploit more ruthlessly and thoroughly than organised workers will allow.

Right now, as the world working class grows rapidly, capital enjoys many options. Labour in many places can be absolutely and relatively forced to provide more and still more surplus value—a factor *definitely* counteracting the tendency of the rate of profit to fall. Add to this that v can be lowered by the reduction of the workforce, or by the reduction of wages, and we begin to glimpse the battery of approaches open to capital in its effort to avert the **crises** which threaten as **crises**.

17. LABOUR-POWER AND CLASS STRUGGLE

Speaking of the value of labour-power raises several related questions. To begin with, how can we say how much labour-time is 'socially required' to reproduce labour-power?

It is clear that most working people live not at the level of bare subsistence required for simple biological survival, but at a level of subsistence defined *socially*. What workers need is not determined by nature alone, but by social custom. An historical, social, and moral element is present in the definition of the value of labour-power.

Vitally, therefore, the antagonism between capital and labour expresses itself in conflict over just how much workers require. When the working class is strong in particular regions or countries, workers can enforce a relatively higher standard of living—a relatively higher value of labour-power—than in places where they are weak.

This reveals several basic facts. On the one hand, we are reminded of the reality that value is not *natural, but social*—people *treat* some labour product as a commodity, *making* the labour going into the commodity 'abstract, socially standard.'

SINCE LABOUR IS 'ABSTRACT' NOT MATERIALLY BUT AS A RESULT OF SOCIAL PRACTICE, WE CANNOT MEASURE ITS MAGNITUDE WITH A CLOCK. HOW MUCH 'ABSTRACT LABOUR-TIME' GOES INTO A COMMODITY IS, INDEED, BASED ON A CALCULATION OF REAL LABOUR-TIME, BUT AVERAGE LABOUR-TIME IS SOMETHING ABSTRACT.

The social nature of value is never more strikingly clear than in the case of the value of labour-power. Though people are generally agreed that workers should be paid 'a living wage'—'enough to lead a decent life'—'enough to keep the wolf away from the door'—*in other words, enough to buy life's basic necessities so that labour-power may be reproduced*—it is *not* generally agreed how much 'a living wage' is. This is a matter of judgement—and struggle!

Always, Moneybags declares a 'living wage' to be less than workers want. If free of opposition, Moneybags will gleefully lower wages to the level of bare subsistence—and even lower, counting on public relief to 'make up the difference' (using tax money taken from better-paid sectors of the working class to finance this relief). The only way capital's effort to impoverish workers can be reversed is by the self-organisation of workers—to stop Moneybags dead in his tracks, wrestle him down, and force higher wages.

KEN SPRAGUE

The actual value of labour-power fluctuates with changes in the relative strength of the contending classes, like a needle on a compass. When Moneybags, Cashbox & Co. prevail, wages are driven down. But when workers unite for self-defence—in unions and political parties, for example— they gain the power to fight back. With strong labour organisations, workers are enabled to fight capital effectively, resisting wage cuts, often winning wage rises.

154

At any given moment, the level of wages reflects the balance of power between capital and labour.

THE FIXATION OF ITS ACTUAL DEGREE IS ONLY SETTLED BY THE CONTINUOUS STRUGGLE BETWEEN CAPITAL AND LABOUR, THE CAPITALIST CONSTANTLY TENDING TO REDUCE WAGES TO THEIR PHYSICAL MINIMUM WHILE WORKING PEOPLE CONSTANTLY PRESS IN THE OPPOSITE DIRECTION. THE QUESTION RESOLVES ITSELF INTO A QUESTION OF THE RESPECTIVE POWERS OF THE COMBATANTS.

When working people are powerful enough to put the fear of labour into capital, they push wages up. But capital has many resources. Sly as a fox, and no angel—with no mercy in his heart, and his heart in his wallet—a wondrous thing!—Moneybags relies on many strategems. Forced to pay high wages in one place, Moneybags will invest elsewhere to secure 'cheap labour,' that is, labour power requiring less socially average labour for its reproduction than the labour-power of better paid workers.

If workers in one part of the world accept a 'living standard' lower than that of workers elsewhere, the higher standard can be directly challenged—Moneybags will simply hire cheap rather than expensive labour-power, forcing better paid workers to moderate their wage demands (if they desire to keep their jobs).

156

This is merely one example of competition between workers—competition between sellers of labour-power, who, like all sellers, must keep their prices 'competitive' if they hope to sell.

Sometimes, capitalists will accede to relatively high wage payment: to encourage worker loyalty when profits are high, to divide higher from lower paid workers, or to hire workers with special skills. But never is this done altruistically. *Moneybags wants surplus value*, and surplus value is the difference between the value of labour-power— represented by wages—and the value of the labour *product*— represented by price. All else being equal, the lower the wages, the higher the profits. Moneybags wants low wages!

157

Competition between workers is exploited to the fullest. This is one of the primary factors, in fact, accounting for the dividedness of the world proletariat. Capital has it both ways: when workers in one place (the US, for example) obtain relatively high wages, their employers use every trick in the book to undercut this high pay—above all, by pitting well-paid US workers against foreign 'cheap labour,' seeking to reduce US wages by investing capital in foreign countries. At the same time, with the trumpet blasts of hired politicians, they demand the loyalty of US workers 'to God and country'. Their argument? That workers in the US are better off than elsewhere!

LONDON: CASUAL CATERING WORKERS, MANY OF THEM FOREIGN, SLEEP OUT IN CARDBOARD BOXES AT THE EMPLOYMENT OFFICE

Moneybags is all too happy to have his cake and eat it, too ... to drive US *wages* down by hiring cheaper labour-power available elsewhere, while mobilising US *workers* to fight in wars and 'police actions' designed to quash the revolts of the foreign poor.

So the question of imperialism arises.

For a variety of reasons the capitalists of one nation find it desirable to invest in other, usually poorer nations. Fresh markets, investment opportunities, cheap labour-power and cheap resources are available, to say nothing of coveted political and military influence. When these assets are jeopardised by the agressive self-organisation of the poor and oppressed in these countries,

Moneybags calls upon the poor and oppressed of his own homeland to combat the insurgency. Serving as the basic pool from which soldiers may be drafted into imperialist armies, the workers of the imperialist powers are thus doubly important to capital. Fear and dislike of the foreign poor must be cultivated. Though largely psychological in origin and effects, this fear and dislike nonetheless has a basis as well, in the *competition* between workers.

The usually better paid workers of the great powers prize their relative affluence. They fear the reduction of the value of their labour-power which the competition of poorer foreign workers threatens. Jealously eager to preserve their hard-won pay gains—as well they should be!—better paid workers too often direct their fire not against Moneybags and his fellow capitalists—the enemy—but against poorly paid workers in other lands, viewed as competitors.

This allows Moneybags the best of both worlds—to *militarily* repress the low paid and *economically* contain the better paid.

And more's the pity—because it is only the *alliance* of workers from all lands that can put a stop to predatory capitalism, reaffirming the human needs and capacities that capital alienates and distorts.

SOUTH AFRICAN MINERS

18. ABOLITION OF WAGE-LABOUR

So far, all our talk has been about *labour-power as a commodity*—bought and sold, turning into *alienated labour* when exercised under the thumb of a capitalist's alien, profit-oriented will. We have seen that the value of that remarkable commodity, labour-power, is an issue of permanent interest to capital and labour, as capitalists bend every effort to cheapen labour-power while workers try to increase its value.

BUT RARELY IS THE DEEPER QUESTION ASKED: WHY SHOULD LABOUR-POWER BE A COMMODITY AT ALL? WHY SHOULD CAPITALISTS CONTROL THE EXERCISE OF LABOUR-POWER, GIVING RISE TO ALIENATED LABOUR AND SURPLUS VALUE —

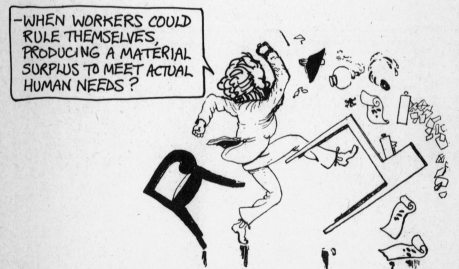

—WHEN WORKERS COULD RULE THEMSELVES, PRODUCING A MATERIAL SURPLUS TO MEET ACTUAL HUMAN NEEDS?

Nor is the ultimate answer to this question often grasped: That workers can seek not merely to elevate the value of labour-power , but to abolish its status as a value. The ability to work does *not* have to be a commodity with a particular exchange-value, sold for wages. Rather, living labour-power—real working people—may unite for democratic, nationless, sexually equal cooperative production, *production for shared use.* This would be *communism* in the authentic sense of the word—ordinary working people democratically in control both of production and the rest of social life, producing for use, not exchange and profit.

Freedom and power for working people would be the hallmark of communist society—a society without bosses of any kind.

WORKING PEOPLE SHOULD NOT BE EXCLUSIVELY ABSORBED IN THE UNAVOIDABLE GUERRILLA FIGHTS INCESSANTLY SPRINGING UP FROM CAPITAL'S NEVER-CEASING EFFORTS TO CUT WAGES AND JOB SECURITY, ITS ATTACKS ON UNIONS, ETC. WORKERS SHOULD UNDERSTAND THAT, WITH ALL THE MISERIES IT IMPOSES, THE CAPITALIST SYSTEM ENGENDERS PRODUCTION SO POWERFUL THAT A NEW SOCIETY OF MATERIAL ABUNDANCE AND SOCIAL FREEDOM IS POSSIBLE. INSTEAD OF THE CONSERVATIVE MOTTO 'A FAIR DAY'S WAGE FOR A FAIR DAY'S WORK!', WORKERS SHOULD INSCRIBE ON THEIR BANNER THE REVOLUTIONARY WATCHWORD —

In reality, workers are *not* paid for their 'labour'—nor is there such a thing as a 'fair wage.' Capitalist production is based on *exploitation*.

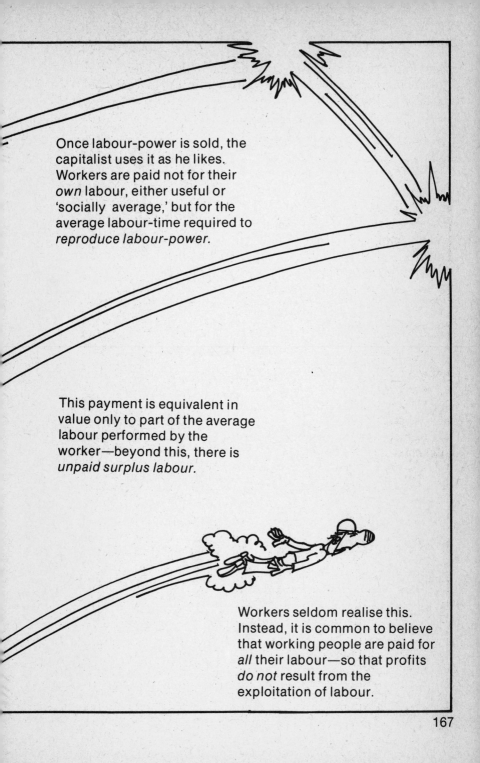

Once labour-power is sold, the capitalist uses it as he likes. Workers are paid not for their *own* labour, either useful or 'socially average,' but for the average labour-time required to *reproduce labour-power*.

This payment is equivalent in value only to part of the average labour performed by the worker—beyond this, there is *unpaid surplus labour*.

Workers seldom realise this. Instead, it is common to believe that working people are paid for *all* their labour—so that profits *do not* result from the exploitation of labour.

The wage-form thus extinguishes every trace of the division of the working day into necessary labour and surplus labour, into paid and unpaid labour. All labour appears as paid labour'.

FEUDAL LABOUR

Under the *corvée* system, in feudal times, it is different. There the labour of the serf for himself, and his compulsory labour for the lord of the land, are demarcated very clearly both in time and space.

SLAVE LABOUR

In slave labour, even the part of the working day in which the slave is only replacing the value of his own means of subsistence, in which he therefore actually works for himself alone, appears as labour for his master. *All* his labour appears as *unpaid* labour.

WAGE LABOUR

In wage-labour, on the contrary, even surplus labour, or unpaid labour, appears as paid.

The exchange between capital and labour seems just like the sale of any commodity. The sale itself seems preordained. After all, reasons the worker,

IT IS THE -UH- **NATURE** OF LABOUR, TO SELL!

It attracts money naturally, and inevitably. The sale of labour-power resulting in the alienation of labour appears to be a datum of nature, unalterable by human intervention. And what appears to sell is not labour-power, but labour.

Fetishism—the belief that labour-power's commodity status is an immutable fact of life—is thus coupled with a misperception of the commodity itself that disguises the reality of exploitation.

DON'T TALK TO ME ABOUT FETISHISM!

Since workers are paid *after* they work, it seems that it is their *work,* not their *ability* to work, which is purchased. Moreover, working people imagine that it is natural for labour-power to sell. 'What else is possible?' This is *fetishism:* the perception that the commodity is intrinsically exchangeable.

169

Like all other commodities, 'labour' seems to have a certain natural exchange-value— a natural price. Hence the widespread faith in that phantom, 'a fair day's wage for a fair day's work.' The truth of the matter is that the unicorn is more common—or the dragon, the griffin, the leprechaun, the kind-hearted corporation and the honest politician.

But people don't usually realise this. Thinking that labour *must* sell as a commodity because this is its *nature*, workers hope for nothing more than a fair wage. In this way they mistake exploitation for nature, seeing no chance for real, unalienated freedom and power.

All the notions of justice held by both the worker and the capitalist, all the mystifications of the capitalist mode of production, all capitalism's illusions about freedom, all the apologetic tricks of vulgar economics, have as their basis the appearance that wages are 'natural' and potentially 'fair.'

WHY DON'T YOU STOP READING THIS BOOK NOW AND SWITCH ON THE T.V.?

They are not, nor can they be. It is not 'natural' for workers to be divorced from the means of production. This, we have seen, is the result of an agonising and bloody historical process—that of *expropriation*. Labour-power is sold to capital only because capital possesses a monopoly on the means of production. So-called 'free workers'—who are free above all to alienate their labour for the privilege of exploitation—experience a travesty of freedom.

171

Without capital—without bosses empowered by the possession of money to buy and control labour-power—workers could genuinely be free. It would once again be possible to combine labour power and means of production *organically*, directly. No sale of either labour-power or means of production would transpire.

Democracy *between* workers, rather than the tyranny of capital *over* workers, would become possible. Collective labour-power—workers united—would freely associate for cooperative control of the means of production.

This requires the self-organisation of the working class for the revolutionary overthrow of capitalism—for an end to commodity production—for the defeat of imperialism and the capitalist state—for the creation of a new and truly free system.

Some lessons about the possible meaning and likelihood of socialist revolution can be gleaned from a renewed look at the Paris Commune, prototype of proletarian self-rule.

Though revolutionary struggle is immensely difficult—the Paris Commune, don't forget, was defeated, and France, a century later, remains capitalist—the possibilities are no less immense. The past century has witnessed the spread of revolutionary politics among workers the world over, so that, in France, for example, millions of workers view themselves as socialists, enemies of exploitation. This is true of many other countries, too, and even where class consciousness is little developed, its potentialities remain vast.

Working class parties and trade unions are necessary for working people to act in concert, whether for self-defence or self-emancipation. No one can 'give' socialism to the working class. Socialism has no possible meaning for working people as the idea of a 'new boss, same as the old boss'. Socialism, as **Rosa Luxemburg** observed, is not some sort of Christmas present for the worthy people who put up with a dictatorship *over* the workers in the name of the workers. Rather, socialism must be the *self-emancipation* of working people: the conquest of power *for* workers *by* workers, by means of the development and exercise of working class power.

STALIN

DON'T LISTEN TO HER!

ONLY THE WORKING CLASS, BY ITS SELF-ACTIVITY, CAN BRING ABOUT SOCIALISM. THAT MEANS **WORKERS CONTROL.** NOBODY CAN BRING ABOUT SOCIALISM 'ON YOUR BEHALF'...

ROSA LUXEMBURG

If the proletariat isn't united, self-active, and resolute, it will be unable to break capital's stranglehold. No 'substitute' for the proletariat can be found. If exploitation is to end, it must be the exploited who end it. Politically organised—in revolutionary parties and geographic or industrial councils—workers must take their fate into their own hands.

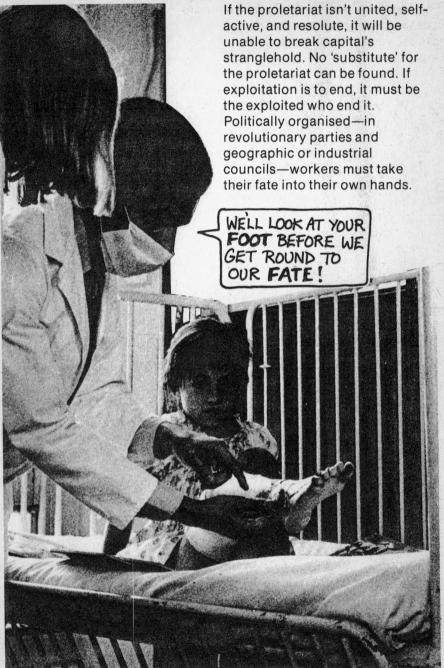

177

This is what happened in Paris, in 1871, with the formation of the Commune. Though the radical democracy and cooperation of the revolutionary Paris uprising didn't last—it was crushed by force of arms—the spirit and aims of the Communards radiated outwards to tens and hundreds of millions in the decades which followed.

Some Paris revolutionaries— **Blanqui,** for example—had elitist misconceptions about what the revolution portended. Though an admirable and indomitable agitator, Blanqui failed to see that the proletariat must organise *as a class* for revolutionary change.

BLANQUI SPENT 45 YEARS IN FRENCH PRISONS.

SINCE BLANQUI CONCEIVES OF EVERY REVOLUTION AS THE **COUP DE MAIN** OF A SMALL REVOLUTIONARY MINORITY, WHAT FOLLOWS OF ITSELF IS THE NECESSITY OF DICTATORSHIP AFTER ITS SUCCESS – THE DICTATORSHIP, PLEASE NOTE, NOT OF THE ENTIRE REVOLUTIONARY CLASS, THE PROLETARIAT, BUT OF THE SMALL NUMBER WHO MADE THE **COUP DE MAIN** AND WHO LIKEWISE ARE ORGANISED BEFOREHAND UNDER THE DICTATORSHIP OF ONE OR A FEW INDIVIDUALS.   <u>ENGELS</u>

I HOPE YOU'RE NOT REFERRING TO **ME**, ENGELS!

179

When big groups and the class itself are unavailable for action, small groups must organise. But the goal of organising must be proletarian *self*-emancipation and *self*-rule. A small dictatorial group exploiting the working class is no better than a class of private capitalists exploiting the working class. What is required is an uprising like the Paris Commune, but on an infinitely greater, broader, more sustained scale—for the abolition of the wage and commodity system.

THE EXPROPRIATORS
ARE EXPROPRIATED

'With the entanglement of all peoples in the net of the world market–and with this, the growth of the international character of the capitalist regime– there arises a world proletariat, *and a growing revolt of the proletariat. This exploited class, prevented by capital from realising its potential for freedom and unrestrained productivity, may yet oppose itself to the capitalist integument. This integument is burst asunder. The knell of capitalist private property sounds. The expropriators are expropriated.'*

and that's not all folks!

Next comes freedom.

ABOLITION OF WAGE-LABOR: Basic goal of the socialist workers' movement. Taking control over the labor process away from the capitalist class, so that working people may collectively and democratically organise production, distribution, and all social life.

ABSOLUTE SURPLUS VALUE: See "Surplus Value".

ABSTRACT LABOR: Essence of value (and hence, the leading social reality of capitalist society.) Useful labor rendered socially "abstract" when treated as "average, equal labor" —sans qualities, and thus only quantitatively comparable — for purposes of exchange.

ACCUMULATION OF CAPITAL: Basic function and tendency of capital to "self-expand" by the exploitation of working people. Invested in means of production and labor-power, capital extracts surplus value from labor to permit its own expanded reproduction (the reproduction, i.e.,of pre-existing capital *coupled* with the production of new capital). The central dynamic of capitalist society.

ALIENATED LABOR: The exercise of labor-power performed under the control of an alien social force (e.g. a slave-owner, feudal aristocrat, capitalist, or production bureaucrat.) Denotes either the alienated *laborer* or the main contemporary *class* of alienated laborers, the proletariat.

ALIENATION: Placing some human power or product under

the domination of an alien entity, either by surrender (allowing a boss control over labor-power), by omission (allowing the economy dominion over humankind by failing collectively to "master the production process"), or by projection (investing deities and charismatic authorities with powers actually inherent in ordinary people.) There are many types of alienation, only some of which are relevant here.

ALIENATION OF NEED: Conversion of the human wealth of needs into a narrow need for wealth. One result of the emergence of money as the commodity universally equivalent for all others. Integral to the profit-motive, and to the "accursed hunger" for money generally.

ALIENATION OF USEFUL LABOR: Conversion of useful labor into abstract labor. The process by which the concrete, useful qualities of labor are disregarded for purposes of exchange. Opens the door to all kinds of abuse of labor.

ALIENATION OF USE-VALUE: Conversion of qualitatively useful objects and entities into "forms of value", as "exchange-values". Process by which the tangible properties of useful labor-products are disregarded for purposes of exchange.

ANARCHY OF PRODUCTION: One central feature of the capitalist division of labor, in which each producer or firm, acting as a private unit, engages in production and exchange uncoordinated by collective planning.

ANARCHISM: Social philosophies advocating pure independence for every individual. May be nostalgically pro-capitalist (urging "laissez faire" or "perfect competition"), utopian semi-socialist (à la Proudhon, urging private commodity production without money or capital), or genuinely socialist (emphasising the libertarian essence of proletarian self-rule).

ARISTOCRACY: A land-owning class — either slave-owning (as in Antiquity, or, more recently, Brazil and the United States); employing serf labor (as in feudal Europe and Japan); or semi-capitalist (as in many countries today, relying partly on hired labor).

BOURGEOISIE: The class of private owners of capital, buying labor-power to allow the expanded reproduction of capital.

CAPITAL: The highest value-form; money invested to generate extra money. Expended in two principal forms: as *variable capital*, for the purchase of labor-power; and as *constant capital*, for the purchase of means of production. By extracting surplus value from the exercise of labor-power, capital accumulates, becoming "self-expanding value".

CAPITALISM: The mode of production resting on systematic commodity production. Involves production under the aegis of capital — production both for exchange and for profit, based on the exploitation of labor following the sale of labor-power. *Private capitalism:* competition between profit-seeking firms controlled by members of the bourgeoisie. *State capitalism:* production-for-profit by state enterprises controlled by members of the state bureaucracy.

CAPITALIST CLASS: Under conditions of private capitalism, the bourgeoisie; under conditions of state capitalism, the state bureaucracy.

CLASS STRUGGLE: Every struggle by contending social classes for control over labor-power and means of production. Also, class contests for political and cultural hegemony — the *means* by which power over the labor process may be assured.

CAPITALIST DIVISION OF LABOR: A world system of anarchic, uncoordinated production, with "units of capital" ranging from the microscopic (small employers) to the gigantic (multinational firms and state enterprises) in fierce, often violent competition.

CIRCULATION: The process of commodity exchange, involving the transfer and metamorphosis of "value-forms" (commodities, money, and capital). Two major "circuits" of capitalist circulation exist: for workers, labor-power sells for money, allowing the purchase of commodities; while, for capitalists, capital buys commodities (including labor-power), allowing capital accumulation.

CLASS SOCIETY: Every society in which the labor-power of one or more social classes is regularly controlled by others. By monopolising the means of production, exploiting classes deny exploited classes free access to tools, machines, raw materials, and land. Only under conditions of alienation — under the control of an exploiter — are the exploited granted access to means of production.

CLASSLESS SOCIETY: See "Communism".

COMMODITIES: Any useful object or entity produced for exchange. An "exchange-value" as well as a "use-value"; indeed, the most elementary exchange-value. Springing from the alienation of useful labor, commodities are the original units of abstract labor (value). Higher forms of value (money and capital) are more developed commodities ("universal" and "self-expanding", respectively).

COMMODIFICATION: Conversion of use-values into exchange-values.

COMMODITY EXCHANGE: The act by which labor-products change hands, based on calculations of abstract, socially required labor-time. When two products are adjudged to embody equal sums of labor, *they become equivalent*, and hence, *exchangeable*. One now takes the place of the other, allowing the emergence and expansion of commodity production.

COMMODITY PRODUCTION: Production not just for use but for exchange. *Petty* commodity production occurs when products are more-or-less accidentally and irregularly produced for exchange. *Generalised* commodity production emerges when production for exchange becomes so widespread that a special representative commodity (designated "money") now intervenes in the exchange of every other commodity. *Systematic* commodity production (capitalism) prevails when money is used to purchase labor-power for the extraction of surplus value.

COMMUNISM: A society without class domination — without the alienation or exploitation of labor — without classes. *Primitive communism* existed prior to class society, when production for subsistence made exploitation infeasible. *Advanced Communism* — based on high rather than low development of labor-power — will exist only if the exploited prove capable of putting an end to class exploitation. Historically, this has been the ultimate objective of the socialist workers' movement.

COMPETITION: The struggle between units of capital for access to markets, means of production, labor-power, and profits. As sellers of labor-power, workers also compete: for jobs, prerogatives, etc.

CONCRETE LABOR: See "Useful Labor".

CONSTANT CAPITAL: The portion of capital expended for means of production, as opposed to that spent for labor-power (*variable* capital). Called "constant" because means of production add no more value to the product than they themselves contain.

DIALECTICS: A method of analysis focusing on the oppositions internal to phenomena — seeing the commodity, for example, as a contradictory unit of value and use-value. Developed principally by the philosopher, Hegel.

DICTATORSHIP OF THE PROLETARIAT: Socialism, the political rule of the working class following a successful proletarian revolution — strictly a transitional stage, intermediate between capitalism and communism.

DIVIDENDS: The portion of profit awarded to private shareholders in capitalist firms, for personal use rather than investment.

ECONOMIC CRISIS: The inborn tendency of a commodity economy to witness a fall in the rate of profit as a result of the rising organic composition of capital.

EXCHANGE: See "Commodity Exchange."

EXCHANGE-VALUE: The "form" of value in which abstract labor (not usually perceptible *per se*) shows itself to economic actors. Abstract labor appears not *in itself*, but as the product's value in relation to other products — as the product's value *in exchange*. Each of the three principal value-forms — commodities, money, and capital — thus manifests "exchange-value".

EXPROPRIATION: Transfer of control by forcible seizure. The small peasantry, for example, was expropriated when driven from land by profit-seeking nobles. The capitalist class also faces the prospect of expropriation — at the hands of socialist workers.

FETISHISM: *Not* the Freudian concept (attraction to substitute sexual objects). Rather, the belief that labor products are imperishably endowed with active value-properties — equivalence, exchangeability, and the initiative that propels exchange. The belief that the *system* of commodified labor-products (the capitalist economy) is irresistibly "out of control", initiating economic change "with the mastery over man", rather than vice-versa.

FETISHISATION: The cognitive structuring of perception so that commodities and systematic commodity production appear to possess alien powers naturally and unalterably.

FEUDALISM: The mode of production directly succeeding slavery and (in Europe) preceding capitalism. Based on the exploitation of serf labor by seigneurial nobles, through coerced surplus labor performed on the lord's land.

FREE ASSOCIATION OF PRODUCERS: The heart of communism — radical democracy among producers freely collaborating for common, mutually determined ends, in lieu of class domination. The free, collective self-determination of labor-power.

INDEPENDENT PRODUCERS: Small commodity producers, selling either self-made material commodities or commodified labor services. Not capitalists because they do not buy labor-power; not proletarians because they do not *sell* labor-power.

INTEREST: See "Surplus Value".

INVESTMENT: The productive expenditure of capital for means of production and labor-power to allow the generation of commodities. Intended to produce surplus value, and hence, capital.

LABOR: See "Useful Labor". Also denotes the modern *class* of laborers, the proletariat.

LABOR-POWER: The capacity to labor. In the economic sense, the capacity to "produce" (to use means of production); broadly defined, the capacity to *create*, i.e., to expand not only productivity, but culture.

LABOR-TIME: The time required for the production of a labor product. When labor-power is exercised usefully for the production of a use-value, labor-time is concrete — i.e., the actual number of hours and minutes expended in production. When, by contrast, labor-power is exercised abstractly for purposes of exchange, labor-time, too, is abstract; instead of comprising concrete labor-time, the labor-time going into production for exchange is *abstract* labor-time, a certain quantity of "socially required labor".

MATERIALISM: The philosophical stance emphasising the centrality and ultimate actuality of "the material" vis-à-vis "the ideal". Ludwig Feuerbach, following the lead of such characteristic Enlightenment thinkers as Helvetius and Holbach, initiated an important materialist critique of Hegel. Marx accepted this, stressing that human ideas, intentions, and initiatives *arise from* — and confront — *pre-existing* situations that place limits on the outcomes of human action. Hardly a "mechanical materialist", however, Marx posited a reciprocal relation between subjectivity and objectivity — in which subjectivity, though pre-shaped by objective circumstances, may yet reshape both its environments and itself (within historically given limits).

MEANS OF PRODUCTION: Any use-value or set of use-values employed in the labor process. All implements, machines, raw materials, lands, even natural forces (e.g., rivers harnessed for the generation of hydroelectric power) that may be used during the exercise of labor-power for the production of an expanded stock either of use-values or exchange-values.

MEANS OF SUBSISTENCE: Any use-value or set of use-values available for the reproduction of labor-power. "Necessities", generally, are primary, while "luxuries" are secondary. (Note what is considered "necessary" varies across time and space. There is no absolute criterion; rather, we refer to "socially necessary means of life".)

MODES OF PRODUCTION: Definite production relations structured on the basis of particular forms of exploitation, involving distinct applications of labor-power to means of production.

Capitalism, feudalism, and slavery are classic modes of production.

MONEY: The second of the three major forms of value — specifically, "the universal equivalent value-form". Both the commodity universally exchangeable for all others, and "self-expanding value" when, as capital, money purchases labor-power and means of production for the generation of surplus value (via the exploitation of labor).

MONOPOLY: Control of the production of some commodity by one unit of capital (a firm, state enterprise, or private owner). Emerges from and restricts competition.

NECESSARY LABOR: The total labor socially required to reproduce the labor-power. Any labor beyond this is *surplus* labor. In *non-commodity production*, both necessary and surplus labor are *useful*. In capitalism, however, necessary labor is *abstract* — the sum of abstract labor equivalent to the abstract labor embodied in labor-power as a commodity. Thus, necessary labor produces values equivalent to the value of the labor-power of which it is, itself, the exercise. *Surplus* labor produces surplus *value*.

ORGANIC COMPOSITION OF CAPITAL: The union, in some ratio, of constant and variable capital as the basic elements of the capitalist production. If constant capital is "c" and variable capital "v", the organic composition of capital = c/v. When c rises in relation to v — when the proportion of productive capital spent for means of production rises relative to that spent for labor-power — the organic composition of capital is said to rise. When the converse occurs, it is said to fall. According to Marx, it is the historic tendency of capitalism for c to rise faster than v.

OVERPRODUCTION: The production of so many commodities that prices and profits fall to levels unacceptable to capitalists, inspiring production cuts.

PARTICULAR EQUIVALENT FORM: Some particular commodity identified by a producer as the value equivalent of the product s/he produces. Money, by contrast, is the *universal* value equivalent, identifiable in some proportion as the equivalent of *every* producer's commodity. Gold, originally just a particular equivalent, later became the money commodity, universally equivalent to all others.

PEASANTRY: A class of small agricultural producers, either independent (free farmers) or dependent and exploited (feudal serfs).

PETTY BOURGEOISIE: From the French — literally, class of small private producers. May denote several different strata: independent producers (including free farmers); small private sellers of commodified labor services (lawyers, doctors, plumbers); and small capitalists employing a handful of workers. A composite and much abused term, seldom clearly defined.

PRICE: The value of commodities expressed in money terms. Value's principle appearance-form in capitalist society — given that every commodity (including labor-power) expresses its value in exchange, by means of a price.

PRICE OF LABOR-POWER: The wage-form of the value of labor-power. Wages *appear* to be the price, not of labor-power, but of labor. This obscures exploitation — for if labor is *paid for*, where does an unpaid surplus come from ? Not, evidently, from labor, but from capital. Actually, not labor but labor-power is purchased; and the labor this allows then generates not only labor-power's value equivalent, but *surplus* value, as well.

PRIMITIVE COMMUNISM: See "Communism".

PRIVATE CAPITALISM: See "Capitalism".

PRIVATE PROPERTY: The legal foundation of capitalism; specifically, systematic commodity ownership by private individuals. Important above all is private ownership *by capital* of the means of production and labor-power. *Personal* ownership of means of subsistence is subsidiary but implicated in capitalist property relations, given that class inequality limits not only free access to means of production, but also to means of life.

PRODUCTION FOR USE: The adaptation of objects and objective situations to non-monetary human needs by the creative exercise of labor-power; thus, the guiding activity of every mode of reproducing labor-power and culture.

PRODUCTION FOR EXCHANGE: Commodity production, in which production for use is eclipsed as labor's central purpose. Though every exchange-value must also possess use-value (or appear to) if it is to sell, exchange-values are nonetheless *alienated* as use-values when they are produced not directly for use, but for value exchange.

PRODUCTION FOR PROFIT: *Capitalist* commodity production, in which the exploitation of the creative exercise of labor-power is the guiding activity. A subset of production for exchange.

PRODUCTION RELATIONS: Social relations pivoting around the utilisation of means of production and labor-power. In capitalist society, comprised mainly of relations between capitalists and workers based on capitalist *control* over means of production and labor-power; distinct from *exchange-relations* (the *sale* of labor-power and other commodities).

PROFIT: See "Surplus Value".

PROLETARIAT: The working class of capitalism, exploited in the process of production-for-profit after selling labor-power to capital. Both the source and, potentially, the "gravedigger" of capitalist relations.

RATE OF PROFIT: Surplus value divided by total capital (constant plus variable capital). With surplus value = s, constant capital = c, and variable capital = v, the rate of profit is $s/c+v$

RATE OF SURPLUS VALUE: Surplus value divided by variable capital. With surplus value = s and variable capital = v, the rate of surplus value is s/v.

RENT: See "Surplus Value".

REPRODUCTION OF LABOR-POWER: The fundamental material and spiritual necessity of human life. The expenditure of creative energy for its renewal through the production and consumption of means of subsistence. May be culturally organised in myriad ways. Capitalism has encouraged a family structure in which the husband trades labor-power for money, so that the wife may exchange money for means of subsistence for the family.

REVOLUTION: The overthrow of a ruling class by a subordinate class. More profoundly radical when a *social system* is overthrown, as well. The proletarian revolution promises the most radical possibility — the abolition of *all* class rule joined with the overthrow of capitalism.

SERFDOM: The classic feudal mode of exploitation in which surplus useful labor is directly extracted from coerced serf labor.

SLAVERY: The classic pre-feudal mode of exploitation, characteristic especially of Antiquity, in which slave labor-power and all its fruits belong directly to the slave-owner who may dispose of them as he will.

SOCIAL CLASSES: Groups defined by their relations to labor-power and means of production.

SOCIALISM: The political rule of the proletariat — collectively and democratically self-regulating — following the overthrow of the capitalist class. Facilitates the transition to a classless, nationless, non-patriarchal society of freely associated producers (communism).

SOCIALLY REQUIRED LABOR: The average quantity of labor required for the production of a given commodity.

STATE CAPITALISM: See "Capitalism".

SUPPLY AND DEMAND: One aspect of the relationship between commodity production and sales: how much is produced and how much is sold. Tension between these two quantities does not, as bourgeois economists imagine, fix commodity values; it does, however, lead to price fluctuations *around* commodity values.

SURPLUS LABOR: The exercise of labor-power for the production of more labor products than are required for the reproduction of labor-power (in capitalist society, for the reproduction of the *value* of labor-power).

SURPLUS VALUE: The absolute and unvarying objective of capitalist production. Attainable strictly by the exploitation of wage-labor, in two principal forms: *Absolute* surplus value is extracted when the absolute quantity of surplus labor-time is expanded, typically by lengthening the workday or speeding up production; *Relative* surplus value is extracted when necessary labor-time falls relative to surplus labor-time, typically by reductions in the value of labor-power. Surplus value is also *distributed* in three forms: as *Interest, Rent,* and *Profit*. Typically, productive investment involves the expenditure of capital (some borrowed) for the generation of surplus value, with some land and equipment rented. When exploitation results in Z surplus value, this Z is divided three ways: between the money-lender, the landlord, and the productive capitalist. Interest and rent, then, no less than profit, are forms of surplus value.

TENDENCY OF THE RATE OF PROFIT TO FALL: Result of the rising organic composition of capital. Given capitalism's tendency to "revolutionise the means of production", constant capital shows a powerful tendency to rise faster than variable capital. This ascending organic composition of capital leads to a descending rate of profit — since the proportion of value-creating capital *falls* relative to non-value-creating capital.

UNIT OF CAPITAL: Any independent unit of production animated by the profit motive, whether a private capitalist firm or a nationalised state enterprise.

UNIVERSAL EQUIVALENT VALUE-FORM: See "Money".

UNPAID LABOR: See "Surplus Labor".

USEFUL LABOR: The exercise of labor-power. The act by which people change natural objects and situations to allow the fulfilment of human needs and desires. Any labor designed to employ or enhance the tangible, useful properties of use-values.

USE-VALUE: The non-exchange usefulness of any given object, whether a labor product or not.

Definable strictly in terms of human desires. It matters not whether these needs spring from the stomach or from imagination. Denotes both the *property* of usefulness and the object *endowed* with usefulness.

VALUE: The defining principle of capitalist social relations — in *substance*, "abstract labor", which exists, however, only in value's three principal *appearance-forms* (commodity-form, money-form, and capital-form).

THE VALUE OF LABOR-POWER: The labor socially required to reproduce labor-power.

VARIABLE CAPITAL: That portion of total productive capital used to purchase value-creating labor-power.

WAGE-LABOR: Labor performed by proletarians after the sale of labor-power for wages. Also refers to the *class* of wage-laborers, the proletariat.

WAGES: The price of labor-power (though seemingly the price of labor). The money-form of the abstract labor going into both the production and reproduction of labor-power.

WORKING CLASS: See "Proletariat".

FURTHER READING

Writings by Marx

The best translation of **Capital** is by Ben Fowkes and David Fernbach (Penguin & New Left: Vol. 1, 1976; Vol. 2, 1978; Vol. 3, forthcoming). Also see: **A Contribution to the Critique of Political Economy** (Progress: Moscow, 1970), trans. by S.W. Ryazanskaya. This small book is the immediate precursor of **Capital**, unsurpassed even by **Capital** on some key questions of value-theory. Also see: **Grundrisse** (Penguin & New Left: Middlesex, 1973), trans. by M. Nicolaus; **Theories of Surplus-Value**, 3 vols. (Foreign Languages Publishing: Moscow, 1970), trans. by S.W. Ryazanskaya, E. Burns, and J. Cohen; and **Value: Studies by Karl Marx** (New Park: London, 1976), trans. by A. Dragstedt. (Penguin/New Left books are published by Vintage in the US.)

About 'Capital'

Roman Rosdolsky, **The Making of Marx's 'Capital'** (Pluto: London, 1977). Ernest Mandel, **The Formation of the Economic Thought of Karl Marx** (Monthly Review: New York & London, 1971). I.I. Rubin, **Essays on Marx's Theory of Value** (Black & Red: Detroit, 1972). Rosa Luxemburg, **The Accumulation of Capital** (Monthly Review: New York & London, 1968). Diane Elson, **Value** (CSE Books and Humanities Press: London & New York, 1979).

Cultural studies based on 'Capital'

Alfred Sohn-Rethel, **Intellectual and Manual Labor** (MacMillan Press: London, 1978). Michael Taussig, **The Devil and Commodity Fetishism in South America** (University of North Carolina: Chapel Hill, 1980). Dean Wolfe Manders, **Wisdom and Mystification in Everyday Life** (Sociology Dissertation, Brandeis University, 1980; available from University Microfilms).

General Marxism

Klaus Fertig, ed., **Marxism, Communism, and the Western World** (Herder & Herder: New York, 1973), an excellent encyclopedia. Maximilien Rubel and Margaret Manale, **Marx Without Myth** (Harper & Row: New York, 1976), superb overview of Marx's life and ideas Herbert Marcuse, **Reason and Revolution** (Beacon: Boston, 1960), masterful account of Marx's Hegelian ancestry. Hal Draper, **Karl Marx's Theory of Revolution** (Monthly Review Press: New York & London; Vol. 1, 1977; Vol. 2, 1978; Vols. 3 & 4 forthcoming), the best, most comprehensive guide to Marx's politics. Raya Dunayevskaya, **Marxism and Freedom** (Pluto: London, 1971). Bertell Ollman, **Alienation** (Cambridge: Lonodn, 1971). Richard Lichtman, "Marx and Freud, pt. 3: Marx's Theory of Human Nature," **Socialist Revolution**, Vol. 7 No. 6, Nov-Dec 1977. Dick Howard and Karl E. Klare, **The Unknown Dimension: European Marxism Since Lenin** (Basic Books: New York, 1972).
Roman Rosdolsky, **The Making of Marx's 'Capital'** (Pluto: London, 1977). Ernest Mandel, **The Formation of the Economic Thought of Karl Marx** (Monthly Review: New York & London, 1971). I.I. Rubin, **Essays on Marx's Theory of Value** (Black & Red: Detroit, 1972). Rosa Luxemburg, **The Accumulation of Capital** (Monthly Review: New York & London, 1968). Diane Elson, **Value** (CSE Books and Humanities Press: London & New York, 1979).

Other titles in Pantheon's documentary comic-book series:

Marx for Beginners
"I recommend it unreservedly for anyone who wants the rudiments of Marx from an engaging mentor."

Andrew Hacker, *New York Times*

The Anti-Nuclear Handbook
"This high-spirited, well-informed and unabashed work of propaganda is a morbidly amusing work to ponder while waiting for the neighborhood meltdown."
New York Times

Lenin for Beginners
"This book is documentary history at its most exciting and informative."
Washington Post

Freud for Beginners
"The treatment of Freud is rigorous, but watching it unfold is just plain fun."
In These Times

Einstein for Beginners
"This book is well illustrated and thoroughly researched....The presentation of [Einstein's] discoveries is little short of inspired."
Washington Post

Mao for Beginners
"Mao Tse-tung made history....Now his works are finally accessible to the Western masses."
UPI Book Corner

Trotsky for Beginners
"A quick, irreverent and rounded portrait....Beginners will enjoy the book—and so will everyone else."
Charleston Evening Post

Capitalism for Beginners
"A witty and pithy explanation of the ideas that underpin the capitalist system."
Los Angeles Times

And most recently published:

Ecology for Beginners
Darwin for Beginners
Economists for Beginners
Marx's Kapital for Beginners